A TWEEN GIRL'S GUIDE TO FRIENDSHIPS

How to Make Friends and Build Healthy Relationships

The Complete Friendship Handbook for Young Girls

Abby Swift

BEMBERTON
BOOKS

SOMETHING
FOR YOU

Thanks for buying this book. To show our appreciation, here's a **FREE** printable copy of the "Life Skills for Tweens Workbook"

WITH OVER 80 FUN ACTIVITIES **JUST FOR TWEENS!**

Scan the code to download your FREE printable copy

TABLE OF CONTENTS

7   **Introduction**

11   The Value of Friendship

27   Making Friends

43   Navigating Different Personalities

57   Healthy vs. Unhealthy Friendships

71   Overcoming Friendship Challenges

89   Losing Friends and Moving On

105   Bullying and Peer Pressure

121   Navigating Friendships in an Online World

137   Friendships and Changes in Puberty

151   Fostering Kindness and Respect in Friendships

163   **Conclusion**

167   **References**

INTRODUCTION

Have you ever had a friend who just gets you and makes you feel amazing? Imagine if you could have more of those amazing friendships!

Being a tween and teenager can be full of challenges. During this time, you're dealing with a lot: puberty, physical changes, new emotions, and so much more. It's an exciting time, but it can be confusing and uncertain. You might find yourself questioning your friendships or wondering how to build the kind of friendships that support you through these transformative years. You're not alone in facing these challenges.

The truth is that navigating friendships during this stage of your life can be tricky. It's normal to feel a little overwhelmed by the changes in your relationships, the ups and downs in friendships, or the pressure to fit in with certain groups. You might have times when you feel alone or misunderstood, when you're not sure who your real friends are, or when you're dealing with conflicts, jealousy, and other friendship hurdles. Without the right tools, these challenges can affect how you feel about yourself, your happiness, and your well-being.

That's where this book comes in! It's your guide to help you understand and enjoy friendships during the tween and teen years.

In this book, you'll learn about:

- What real friendship looks like

- The different kinds of friends you can have

- How to make new friends and keep your old ones close

- How to spot the difference between healthy and unhealthy friendships

- Tips for managing conflicts and jealousy

- Strategies for dealing with friends growing apart, bullying, and peer pressure

- How to manage digital interactions with friends while staying safe

- Understanding how puberty can impact your friendships

By the end of this book, you'll have the tools and knowledge you need to be a fantastic friend and create strong, supportive friendships that make the ups and downs of growing up a little smoother and a lot more fun.

How to Use This Book

Each chapter covers a different topic. While the book is designed to be read from start to finish, you're welcome to jump around to the sections that interest you the most.

Every chapter includes a case study and an activity to help you put what you've learned into practice. By doing these activities and actively engaging with the content, you can gain hands-on experience and reinforce your understanding, ensuring you get the most out of this book.

Ready to begin this journey towards becoming a great friend and building strong, lasting friendships? Let's get started with the first chapter. Best of luck!

1

THE VALUE OF FRIENDSHIP

As you grow older, your friendships will change — and that's perfectly normal. You might find that your group of friends gets smaller, or your interests might change, and you'll make new friends. Having friends is special at any age, but it becomes even more important as you enter your teenage years. Friends can support you, make you feel like you belong, and help you through tough times.

Friendships are precious, and it's easy to take them for granted. But they're one of the best parts of life. In this chapter, we'll dive into what friendship means and look at the different kinds of friends you might have in your life. Let's start by answering a big question: What does it mean to have a friend, and why is it so important?

What Is Friendship?

A friend is someone you feel close to — someone who's there for you, no matter what. You share a special connection with your friends and can count on them when things get tough. You probably have things in common with your friends, like the same beliefs or values, which strengthen your friendships. We'll talk more about the different kinds of friendships in the next section. But at its core, friendship is about feeling connected to someone and really enjoying the time you spend together.

The Building Blocks of a Friendship

Most friendships are built on four key components. A good friendship will have most of these qualities, even though not every one may have them all. To truly understand friendship, it helps to consider how these four aspects play a role in your connection with people.

1. Shared Interests

Most friendships start through shared interests. Joining a new art class, school, sport, or hobby introduces you to new people interested in the same things you are. This common interest can be a starting point for making connections. Over time, as you discover more shared interests, these acquaintances may bloom into friendships.

Remember that shared interests aren't always what keep a friendship strong. You might discover new interests or outgrow the initial ones that brought you together. But once a strong bond is established, your friendship can flourish even when your shared interests change.

For example, imagine you became friends with someone because you both loved playing soccer. As time passes, you might become interested in different sports or hobbies. That doesn't mean your friendship has to end. True friendships can survive and grow despite changing interests.

2. Mutual Respect

Mutual respect is a must-have in any friendship. It means showing admiration and care for one another and, sometimes, acknowledging that your friend might be better than you at something. A friendship without mutual respect is like a garden without sunlight — it simply cannot grow.

Respect in a friendship means honoring each other's space, privacy, and needs. It also means understanding that your friend has other relationships that are just as important to them.

Have you ever had a friend who was always there for you, respected your privacy, and made you feel valued? How did it make you feel?

3. Trust

Trust is the foundation of any friendship. It means that when you make a promise to your friend, you keep it. Like keeping a secret your friend shared with you, trust involves respecting and protecting each other's privacy.

If trust is broken — for example, if a friend shares your secret — it can shake the foundation of your friendship. Trust is what makes you feel safe and respected. Without trust, there's no openness, and without openness, a friendship cannot truly thrive.

Can you think of a time when someone broke your trust? How did it make you feel? How did it affect your friendship?

4. Understanding

Understanding is the final piece that makes a good friendship. It's all about really "getting" your friend — how they feel, what they're going through — even if it's different from what you're experiencing. It's like putting yourself in your friend's shoes for a while and seeing the world from their point of view. It's not about always knowing the right thing to say, but it's about listening, offering a kind word, or just being a shoulder to lean on when they need it.

Being an understanding friend means being there for your friends when they need you, even if you can't fix the problem. Sometimes, knowing someone is there to listen can make all the difference.

Think about a time when a friend was there for you when you needed it most. How did it make you feel?

Now that we know the building blocks of friendship, how can we tell the difference between a good friend and a not-so-good one? Let's find out.

Good and Bad Friends

Every friend is different, and that's what makes friendships so exciting. But not all friendships are created equal. While some friendships can make you feel on top of the world, others can make you feel down in the dumps. Let's break down what makes a good friend and identify signs that a friendship may not be the best for you.

What does a good friendship look like?

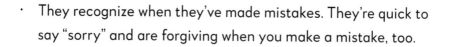

- Good friends support you. They encourage you and cheer you on.

- They make you feel good so you can be yourself.

- They really listen to you. They want to be involved in your life and take an interest in what you're up to.

- They recognize when they've made mistakes. They're quick to say "sorry" and are forgiving when you make a mistake, too.

These types of friends will always make you feel loved and supported. They encourage you to be the best "you" that you can be and inspire you to be a better friend to them and others.

Unfortunately, not all friendships are like this.

Here are some signs of a bad friendship:

- Bad friends gossip about their other friends.

- They only reach out when they want or need something.

- They are pushy — they only care about their opinions and needs.

- They don't accept different opinions.

- They are unreliable. They aren't there when you need them.

Staying in a bad friendship is unpleasant and can affect your health, making you feel drained, stressed, and even anxious. Instead, you need to surround yourself with people who will support and be there for you when things get tough, and you can find these friends in many different areas of your life.

Let's look at the different types of friends you can have.

Different Types of Friends

Just as there are good and not-so-good friendships, there are also different kinds of friends. Having a mix of different types of friends is good, as they bring other things into your life. But remember, you also don't have to have friends in all these categories. Any kind of good friend is an excellent addition to your life! Let's look at three types of friends you might have at different stages in your life.

Best Friends

Best friends are your closest confidants. You trust them with your secrets, dreams, and fears. They support you when times are tough and are there with you to celebrate your wins.

While the strong bonds of best friends are usually built over years of shared experiences, there are times when you might meet someone and instantly feel a deep connection with them. It's almost like you've been best friends for years.

School Friends

School friends are the friends you hang out with at school. Some school friends may also be your best friends, but not always. They could be classmates, teammates, or people you meet at lunchtime. You may be closer to some than others, which is perfectly normal.

As you grow up and your interests change, you may find that you drift apart from some of your school friends. That's totally normal.

Casual Friends

Casual friends are those you're friendly with but not super close to, like people you meet at a summer camp or on vacation. You enjoy spending time with them when you see them, but you don't often plan to spend time with them alone.

Sometimes, a friend of a friend becomes a casual friend. You get along and enjoy their company, but you wouldn't share your deepest secrets with them. Having casual friends is excellent, as these are often friends you can have a lot of fun with and are just nice to be around.

Friends vs. Acquaintances

While you may have a small or large group of friends, chances are you'll have more acquaintances. Acquaintances are people you are friendly with but don't really hang out with. They could be people in school you've known for ages but haven't really hung out with outside school hours, or friends you used to be close with but have drifted apart from. Often, friends start as acquaintances until you get to know them better.

Acquaintances may not be as close to you as friends, but they are still good to chat with when you bump into each other. As you grow up, you'll see the value of having positive relationships with your acquaintances. You never know when you might be able to help each other out.

Now that you've learned what friendship is — the good and the bad — and the different kinds of friends you can have, let's see how this knowledge applies to real life. In the next section, we'll look at a case study of two friends and some questions for you to think about. Then, we'll explore a fun activity to help you understand the different kinds of friends in your life. Let's dive in!

Case Study :

The Lifelong Friendship of Maya and Sophie

Maya and Sophie became best friends in middle school. They both shared a love of art, and spent hours after school doodling in the art room. But when they left middle school, their interests began to change. Maya started playing soccer, while Sophie became interested in drama. Despite these differences, they still hung out regularly and tried to support each other. Sophie always made time to watch Maya's soccer games, and Maya never missed seeing Sophie in her plays.

Their friendship was tested when Sophie moved away for a year due to her parent's work. Initially, this was tricky; with timezone differences to contend with, speaking every day wasn't always possible. Instead, they organized weekly video calls to catch up and share their news. The year flew by, and by the time Sophie returned, their relationship had become even stronger.

After leaving school, their friendship continued to blossom. Despite moving to different parts of the country, they chatted almost every day and met up as often as they could. Recognizing the importance of their friendship, they continued to support each other in every aspect of their lives.

Maya and Sophie's relationship shows the importance and lasting power of best friends. Their lifelong connection is a testament to the timeless nature of true friendship.

Answer the following questions about Maya and Sophie.

1. Maya and Sophie's friendship was initially forged over a love for art. Can you remember how you met your best friend?

At Srcs
2020

2. When Sophie moved away, how did she and Maya keep up their friendship? How can you keep up a friendship with someone who is far away?

They Called frequently!

Call, text, letter, prayer

3. Why do you think Maya and Sophie's friendship strengthened when they were apart for a year?

Because it was tested

4. Maya and Sophie's lifelong friendship changed their lives for the better. Can you share how your friends have changed your life?

They help me grow in
- hope
- love
- faith
- self love

Activity: Friendship Tree

Now that you understand friendships well, it's time to dive into your first activity. You're going to create your very own Friendship Tree. A Friendship Tree is a great way to visualize all the fantastic social connections in your life, with each branch representing a different part of your life and the friends you've made.

Here are the steps:

1. Draw a large tree trunk in the space provided. The main tree trunk represents you, so write your name on it.

2. Next, draw some branches coming out from the main trunk. Each branch represents a different aspect of your life. For example, include a branch for school, one for your hobbies, and another for any other activities. Write the name on the branch.

3. Now, it's time to draw the leaves! Each leaf represents a friend you've made in that part of your life (write their names on the leaves). For instance, any friends you've met at school will be a leaf on your school branch.

The Friendship Tree is a great way to see all of the wonderful friendships you have in your life. Look at your branches, and take a minute to think about all the friends you have and how they add to your life. How do they make you happy? How do they support you? How do they enrich your life? As you get older and explore more hobbies and new opportunities, keep adding new branches to your tree.

Key Takeaways

Friendships are crucial, particularly during your teenage years. They offer support, provide assistance, and fill your life with fun and joy. Friendships come in many forms and from different areas of your life. Remember, not every friend will be your best friend, but each one holds unique value and contributes positively to your life's journey.

MAKING FRIENDS

Making new friends can be a rewarding experience that enriches our lives with diverse perspectives and shared experiences. However, it can also be challenging, especially for those who might feel shy, anxious, or concerned about fitting in. If you want to expand your circle of friends and form stronger bonds with people, you'll need to take proactive steps to overcome these hurdles. In this chapter, we'll provide practical tips to help you approach new people, start conversations, and create meaningful connections.

Whether you already have a large group of friends or not, learning how to approach others and strike up conversations is a valuable life skill that will serve you well beyond your teenage years. But how can you meet new people, start conversations, and make a great first impression?

Approaching New People

Starting a conversation with someone you don't know can be intimidating, regardless of how brave or outgoing you may be. Worrying about saying the wrong thing or not being well-received is natural. Developing the ability to confidently approach new people is a skill you'll use throughout your life. It can help you build stronger relationships, express yourself more effectively, and connect more easily with others.

In most situations, a friendly and genuine approach will be appreciated, and the conversation will flow naturally. The key is to approach others in a way that feels comfortable for you and them. So, how can you do that?

How to Approach New People

You may have noticed that some girls have this amazing ability to make friends with everyone. They confidently walk over to a group of people, and within minutes, everyone's laughing and chatting. If you are one of those girls, that's fantastic! It means you are a people person, and that's a skill that will help you a lot in life. However, if you struggle with approaching new people or striking up conversations, don't worry! In this section, we'll share tips to help you develop your social skills, even if it initially feels challenging.

When you meet and approach new people, there are a few key things to keep in mind that will help you come across as friendly and open. By following these tips, you'll be well on your way to making new friends and forming strong connections.

HOW TO APPROACH NEW PEOPLE

1 **Make Eye Contact**

Show you're listening!

2 **Smile**

Be a friend magnet!

3 **Remember Their Names**

It's like saying "hi" twice!

4 **Ask Open Ended Questions**

Get the chat going!

5 **Find Common Ground**

What do you both ♥?

6 **Show Real Interest**

Listen and Laugh!

Make Eye Contact

Making eye contact is a powerful nonverbal cue that signals your interest in someone. It shows that you are engaged, attentive, and confident. In many cultures, eye contact is also seen as a sign of respect, as it demonstrates that you value and respect the other person.

Remember that you don't have to maintain constant eye contact throughout the conversation. It's okay to look away occasionally, as staring can make the other person feel uncomfortable. Aim for a balance that feels natural and comfortable for both of you.

Smile

A smile goes a long way. If making eye contact makes you uncomfortable, a simple smile is a great way to break the ice. Smiling at someone instantly puts them at ease and makes them more open to conversation. It also makes you seem welcoming and approachable, which can be helpful when you're trying to make new friends.

Remember Their Name

One common mistake when meeting new people is to forget the other person's name. You introduce yourself, they tell you their name, but it doesn't stick, and ten seconds later, you've forgotten it. Everyone does it. But learning people's names when you first meet them is an important skill to develop. When you're able to remember someone's name, it shows them you value them. It's a simple gesture, but it makes a lasting impression.

A simple way to remember a name is to repeat it in your head and use it in your first conversation. For example, if you meet someone called Clare, you might say: "Nice to meet you, Clare!" Then: "What hobbies are you interested in, Clare?" Using the name in the conversation a few times helps reinforce it in your memory.

Another tip is to associate their name with something memorable about them. For example, if you meet someone named Elen who's into soccer, you might mentally associate "Elen" with "soccer." You could even create a nickname like "Soccer-Elen" in your head. This association will help you remember their name the next time you see them.

Ask Open-Ended Questions

Open-ended questions encourage people to share more about themselves and their thoughts. They also show that you're genuinely interested in getting to know them. Unlike simple yes-or-no questions, these questions encourage the person to share more, helping you to get to know them better. Instead of asking someone if they like music, ask them what type of music they enjoy or what they like doing after school.

Here are some more examples of open-ended questions:

- "What do you usually do during summer break?"

- "I noticed you have a Thor badge on your backpack. Have you seen the latest *Avengers* movie? What do you think about it?"

- "What did you think about this morning's history lesson?"

Find Common Ground

Finding common ground with someone is an excellent way to establish a connection. When you share interests or experiences, it gives you something to bond over and talk about.

When you approach a new person, try to look for visual clues. Are they wearing a particular brand of clothes? Do they have unique badges on their backpacks? Do they carry a sports bag? These clues can tell you a lot about a person, making it easier to strike up a conversation and connect over shared interests.

For example, if you notice someone wearing a band t-shirt, you could ask about their favorite songs or concerts by that band.

Remember, the goal is to find topics that both of you enjoy discussing, so be open to exploring various subjects and interests.

Show Real Interest in Them

One of the most important things you can do when talking to someone is show genuine interest in what they say. It's easy to get excited and start talking about yourself, but listening and asking questions about their experiences can make a big difference.

How can you show real interest? It's simple! Listen when they speak, and try not to interrupt. Respond to their words with gestures like nodding, smiling, or showing other emotions. And ask questions to keep the conversation flowing.

Think about a time someone really listened to you. They probably nodded, seemed engaged, and asked you questions, right?

Imagine if that same person had cut you off, only talked about themselves, or seemed distracted.

Remember, making friends is not just about sharing your stories and interests. It's also about getting to know others and showing interest in their lives.

The Importance of Body Language When Meeting New People

Meeting someone new is more than just saying the right things and listening to them talk. Your body language plays a big part, too. Body language is how you use your body to express your feelings and thoughts without words. It includes how you hold yourself, your facial expressions, how you move your hands, and how you sit or stand.

If you slouch, sigh, roll your eyes, or generally appear disinterested when someone is talking, they will pick up on those signals. This might make them uncomfortable and question if you're genuinely interested in getting to know them.

So, how can you make your body language more inviting? Try keeping your arms at your sides instead of crossing them, standing or sitting with a straight back, and looking up at the person. These gestures convey confidence. When you add a warm smile, make eye contact, and nod in agreement, you signal that you are genuinely interested in what they're saying.

Managing Shyness and Fear of Rejection

Even with all the tips you've learned about approaching new people, it's natural to still feel shy. Being shy isn't a bad thing. Some people, called extroverts, love being around others. They enjoy being the center of attention and feel energized in social situations. Introverts, on the other hand, often prefer quieter environments with fewer people. They might find big crowds a bit much and sometimes feel unsure in new environments.

Whether you're an extrovert or an introvert, both are totally normal. And everyone feels shy sometimes in certain situations.

Managing Shyness

Shyness might simply mean feeling uneasy in new situations or around people you don't know. You might feel nervous or anxious around others, particularly when you're the center of attention or being asked questions. While it's normal to feel shy sometimes, it's important to learn how to handle this feeling so you can make new friends and feel more at ease around others.

Remember, it's totally okay to be shy, and you're definitely not the only one who feels this way. However, learning how to manage your shyness is a valuable skill, as you'll often encounter new and unfamiliar situations in life.

Here are a few tips to help manage shyness when meeting new people:

- **Prepare in advance**: If you know you'll be in a situation where you'll meet new people, like joining a club or a new sports team, you could prepare a few questions and answers beforehand. For example, to start a conversation and break the ice, you might say, "Hi, I'm [Your Name], what's yours?" or "I noticed your [book, shirt, etc.], I'm a big fan of that, too!"

- **Practice in the mirror**: Now that you have some questions and answers lined up, instead of imagining how you'll respond, practice in the mirror. Talking to yourself might initially seem strange, but it can help you feel more confident and ready.

- **Find common interests**: It's easier to connect with someone when you have something in common, so try to find those shared interests. Visual cues like the clothes they wear or the bags they carry might give you hints about what they like.

- **It's okay to be shy**: Even the most confident people are shy in certain situations, so feeling shy is perfectly normal. Just try not to let it hold you back from doing what you want.

Managing Fear of Rejection

Sometimes, the thought of talking to new people can be scary because we worry they might not want to be our friends. It's okay to feel this way; most of us do! But remember, just because someone doesn't click with you doesn't mean there's something wrong with you. In fact, they're missing out on getting to know a fantastic person: you!

Life is full of ups and downs, and everyone faces rejection now and then. But guess what? Rejection doesn't define your worth. Think about it: maybe you tried out for the school's hockey team and didn't get in this time. Instead of letting it get you down, use it as fuel to practice harder! When you achieve your goal later on, whether rocking the hockey field or finding a best friend, the joy will be even sweeter.

Keep putting yourself out there, and you'll find the friends and opportunities that are right for you.

Case Study :

The Story of Lucy and Liam

Lucy was a quieter girl at school, who found it tough to meet new people and make friends. Instead of playing outside at break, she preferred to read comics in the classroom. Then, one summer, Liam, a new student, joined the school. Much like Lucy, Liam was shy and enjoyed spending his breaks reading comic books.

When their teacher assigned them a project to create a comic book, Lucy saw this as the perfect opportunity to get to know Liam. Even though Lucy felt nervous about approaching Liam, she knew they shared an interest in comic books already, so that was a fantastic starting point.

After a few weeks of working together on the project, Liam opened up and came out of his shell. Lucy seemed to forget her initial anxiety. The project was a huge success, and fast forward to the end of the school year, and Lucy and Liam had become the best of friends.

The experience had taught Lucy that overcoming her shyness and putting herself out there to make new friends was worth it. It just took a bit of courage and, of course, a lot of comic books!

Answer the following questions about Lucy and Liam.

1. **Can you think of a time when you started a conversation with someone new. What did you talk about? How did you feel?**

   Angie how we ♡ the word
   slayd I felt exited that I'd
   met a new friend!.

2. **What did Lucy and Liam have in common that made it easier to initiate a conversation?**

   They both ♡ Comic books

3. **How did Lucy overcome her shyness when she decided to speak with Liam? Can you think of a time when you overcame similar feelings?**

   When they were Partners
   for a project. When I
   Presented my slides to 4B!

4. **How do you think Lucy's experience changed her confidence? How have your experiences with making friends boosted your confidence?**

   The more you do
   it the easyier it
   bcomes.

Activity: Role-Play Scenarios

In this role-play activity, you will imagine meeting three new friends at school. Each person has unique hobbies and interests. Your job is to engage with these people by asking about their hobbies and seeing if you can find a shared interest. Use the strategies you have learned in this chapter and consider how you will approach these people to make new friends.

You can also involve your family by asking one of them to role-play as the new friend while you practice what you have learned to communicate with them. Ready? Good luck!

Role-play 1: Gemma

Gemma's a new student at your school from Germany. She seems friendly, and you've noticed that she has a patch of Olaf from Frozen on her bag, so you guess she likes Disney. She's also in your art class, so she might like painting.

How could you start a conversation with Gemma?

have you watched the 2nd frozen mone

Role-play 2: Miguel

Miguel is another new student in your
class, and he's just moved here from New
Mexico. He's struggled to get to know the
other kids since joining partway through
the year. He's a bit shy, but you've noticed
he brings a soccer ball to school and rides
a skateboard, so those might be some of
his hobbies.

**What could you say to Miguel to start a conversation and make
him feel more at home?**

Soccer team starts at src in
october are you going to try
out

Role-play 3: Abi

Abi was in your primary school class and
just transferred to your school this year.
You never really talked before and aren't
sure if she remembers you. You know she
likes swimming and the outdoors, since
she talked about it back in primary school.

Talking to Abi might be awkward since you don't know if she remembers you.

What could you say to Abi to break the ice and make her feel welcome?

hi abi Im molly its so
nice to see you do you
remember me?

 Key Takeaways

Making new friends can be daunting. Being shy and worrying about what other people think can make it tough to approach new people and make friends. But remember the tips we've shared: Look people in the eye, ask questions that keep the conversation going, listen when someone's talking, and use friendly body language. Doing these things can help you seem confident, open, and interested in the other person. It will also make it much easier for you to make new friends.

NAVIGATING DIFFERENT PERSONALITIES

Today you are you. That's truer than true.
There's no one alive who is youer than you!
~ Dr. Seuss

Just imagine how boring life would be if we were all the same. If we all thought the same, talked the same, walked the same, and did everything in the same way, the world would lack color, diversity, and fun. Lucky for us, we're all unique, each with our own special personalities — a mix of characteristics and traits that shape how we think, feel, and behave.

Think about your circle of friends. Some might be bubbly, confident, and always up for an adventure, while others might be more reserved and shy. The key is that there's no "right" or "better" personality type. Everyone is different, and embracing this uniqueness and individuality makes life more exciting and fun.

Why Personalities Matter

Understanding and navigating different personalities is a vital part of growing up. Wherever you go, you'll meet people who are different from you. They might look, talk, think, and react differently in certain situations. Even though differences can sometimes cause tension, it's crucial to cooperate with people and even be friends with those different from you.

This chapter will discuss how to understand and navigate different personalities. Before diving into the benefits and challenges of different personalities and viewing a case study, let's first look at the different personality types.

Understanding Personality Types

Your personality is like a puzzle, and each trait is a unique piece that fits together to form the complete picture of who you are. Each part of your personality contributes to making you special.

While it's true that some people are really similar, like siblings, parents, and even friends, no two people are exactly alike — not even twins. Many factors set two people apart from each other, and our personalities are just one of those factors.

As you get older, you'll notice that your friends have different personalities, too. Even though everyone is unique, most people share certain personality traits. Recognizing these personality traits (in others and yourself) is an important part of learning to interact with different personalities.

Researchers and scientists have spent much time figuring out exactly how many personality traits there are. There are many personality theories, and one well-known theory is The Big 5 model, presented by Kendra Cherry in Very Well Mind (2023). According to this model, there are five primary personality traits: agreeableness, openness, extroversion, neuroticism, and conscientiousness.

Let's look at these traits to help you understand yourself and your friends better.

- **Agreeableness**: Agreeable people are friendly, value teamwork, and enjoy helping others. They're great at making friends, but may struggle with low self-esteem and avoid conflict. Have you ever found it hard to say "no?"

- **Openness**: Open people are creative and like trying new things. They adapt well to change and see life as an adventure. But they can sometimes be seen as self-centered or unreliable. Do you like to explore new things?

- **Extroversion**: Extroverted people enjoy being around others and feel energized in social settings. They're often charismatic, but may come across as self-centered. Do you love chatting and sharing stories?

- **Neuroticism**: Neuroticism means being emotional — feeling both joy and sadness intensely. It's not necessarily negative, but these people may overthink and worry a lot. Do you often find yourself worrying about things?

- **Conscientiousness**: Conscientious individuals are responsible and considerate. They're great at planning, but may struggle to relax and let go of control. Are you the one in your group who always remembers everything?

Remember that no one fits perfectly into just one of these categories. Most of us exhibit all of these personality types to varying degrees. At the end of this chapter, you'll take the Big 5 Personality Test to see how you score for each trait.

So, what are the benefits and challenges of different personalities? Let's find out in the next section.

Benefits and Challenges of Different Personalities

No one is perfect, and neither are personality types. But by understanding the benefits and challenges of each personality type, you'll gain valuable insight into your friends. You'll find it easier to navigate the ups and downs of different personalities and build stronger, more meaningful relationships.

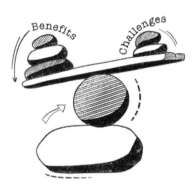

Complementary Personalities

Every personality type has its unique strengths that can complement others. Imagine your friend group as a team, where each member brings something special. An extroverted friend might help an introverted friend come out of their shell. A conscientious friend could ensure everyone stays on track and is never late. An open friend might have fascinating stories to share, while an agreeable friend can help the group make new friends. A friend with high neuroticism will always be open about their feelings, offering a sense of emotional honesty.

Challenges and Conflicts

Of course, blending different personalities can sometimes lead to disagreements. A conscientious person might get frustrated with the carefree attitude of an open friend, and an agreeable friend may find a neurotic friend overwhelming. When conflicts arise, it's crucial to respect each other's differences and work together to find a solution.

Acceptance and Change

Sometimes, you might not agree with your friends, and that's okay. Accept your friends for who they are, even if their personality traits can be challenging. Remember that people's personalities can change over time, and it's important to support and embrace those changes within your friend group.

Now that you understand the different personality types, their benefits and challenges, and their value in a group of friends, it's time to put your knowledge to the test. Complete the case study of Alex, Sandy, and Anika, and take a simplified version of the Big 5 Personality Test to see which personality traits you score high or low in. Good luck!

Case Study:

Alex, Sandy, and Anika

Alex, Sandy, and Anika have been friends since kindergarten. Alex is a thoughtful introvert. She likes reading, being in nature, and spending time with her best friends, Sandy and Anika. Sandy is the complete opposite of Alex. She is loud and outgoing. She loves being around people, going to the shopping mall, and talking to strangers to pet their dogs at the park. Anika is an adventurer at heart. She loves trying new things, often meeting new people along the way.

Despite their differences, the girls have kept their friendship strong and complemented each other well. Alex always thinks of everything—what to bring, when to leave to be on time for the movies, and what potential problems they might encounter. Sandy, on the other hand, is impulsive and often persuades Alex to accompany her to parties. This helps Alex make more friends and come out of her shell more. And everyone can count on Anika to come up with something new (and sometimes crazy) for the girls to do.

Even though their personalities are different, the girls have learned to work together to complement each other's needs in the friendship, and they are always understanding and respectful towards each other.

Answer the following questions about Alex, Sandy, and Anika.

1. Can you spot the different personality types in Alex, Sandy, and Anika? How would you describe each one's personality?

   Alex: Calm
   Sandy: Outgoing
   Anika: Planner

2. How do Alex, Sandy, and Anika's personalities contribute to and strengthen their friendships?

   It wheighs their thoughts and feelings

3. Can you think of a time when personality differences caused a misunderstanding in your friendship group? How was it resolved?

   Yes

4. Alex, Sandy, and Anika all have different personalities. Can you identify the personality traits in some of your friends?

   Tess: Loud, outgoing, humoruos
   Jewle: Calm, funny, Quiet

Activity: Personality Quiz

Here's a test based on the Big 5 personality traits. Please note that this is a simplified version and not a scientifically validated test. It is just for informational and entertainment purposes only.

Instructions: For each statement, indicate the extent to which you agree or disagree by selecting the option that best describes you.

	Strongly Agree	Agree	Neutral	Disagree	Strongly Disagree

1) I am talkative and outgoing

2) I tend to be organized and efficient.

3) I am open to new experiences and enjoy exploring different ideas.

4) I am generally calm and emotionally stable.

5) I am dependable and can be relied upon.

6) I am curious and enjoy learning new things.

7) I tend to be reserved and quiet.

8) I am compassionate and care about others' well-being.

9) I am organized and pay attention to details.

10) I experience a range of emotions and can be easily affected by them.

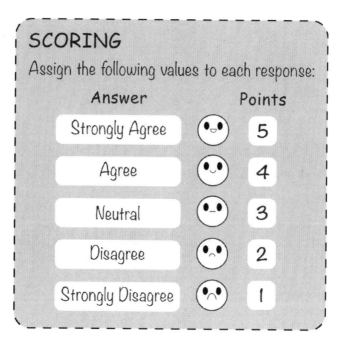

SCORING

Assign the following values to each response:

Answer		Points
Strongly Agree	😄	5
Agree	🙂	4
Neutral	😐	3
Disagree	🙁	2
Strongly Disagree	😞	1

To interpret your results, add up your score for each trait:

Trait	Add Points for Questions	Score
Extroversion	1 & 7	
Conscientiousness	2 & 9	
Openness	3 & 6	
Neuroticism	4 & 10	
Agreeableness	5 & 8	

Now, let's work out your results! The higher your score for a particular trait, the more you exhibit that personality type's characteristics. And if you have a lower score? It simply means those traits aren't as prominent in your personality.

But remember, this is just a bit of fun, and there's no "good" or "bad" in this quiz. It's all about celebrating who you are! Scoring high or low on any trait doesn't mean you're better or worse than anyone else. Instead, it shines a light on the colorful mix of traits that make you uniquely YOU. Embrace your results and enjoy learning more about your awesome self!

 Key Takeaways

Having friends with a mix of personalities can be incredibly rewarding, as your friends will complement each other and ensure balance in a group. However, different personality traits can sometimes lead to friction or conflicts. There are no "good" or "bad" traits; it's simply about understanding and accepting the different personalities.

HEALTHY VS. UNHEALTHY FRIENDSHIPS

Now that you're familiar with the various types of friends and how personalities can complement each other and sometimes clash, let's explore the difference between healthy and unhealthy friendships. Remember, there's a fine line between occasionally disagreeing with a friend and being in an unhealthy friendship.

Friendships are rooted in love and support. In a healthy friendship, there's a balance of give and take. You offer your friends attention, friendship, and support; they do the same for you. If your friends don't respect or support you, it might be time to reevaluate the health of the friendship.

In this chapter, we'll examine the features of a healthy friendship and the red flags that indicate an unhealthy one. After learning about these distinctions, you'll apply your knowledge to a case study on handling an unhealthy friendship and take a friendship checkup activity to assess your current friendships.

Before we get into all of that, let's start at the beginning. What makes a friendship healthy? How can you identify a positive relationship?

Characteristics of Healthy Friendships

Good friends are people you can trust, who support you when you need a helping hand, and whom you enjoy spending time with. We've touched on some aspects of what makes good friends in Chapter 1. They lift you up, make you feel good about yourself, listen to you, aren't afraid to admit when they've messed up, and never hold grudges.

Healthy friendships aren't always smooth sailing. Sometimes, you'll have differences of opinion. When both of you feel strongly about something, it may result in an argument. What matters is how you handle these differences and treat each other afterward.

What makes a good friendship? Here are seven characteristics of healthy friendships:

1. **Mutual Respect:** Respect is at the heart of any healthy friendship. It means honoring each other's personal space, treating your friends in the same way you would want to be treated, and listening to their opinions and views, even if they differ from yours. Mutual respect is the foundation for any healthy friendship.

2. **Trust:** Trust is essential in a strong friendship. Knowing your friends will be there for you when you need them is vital for building a healthy and long-lasting friendship. Trust also extends to secrets. If you share something private, your friend should keep it confidential.

3. **Open Communication:** Open communication is key to understanding each other's boundaries and enhancing trust. It means

that you feel comfortable expressing yourself freely and openly. It also means you can talk about any topic, even if it may be tricky, and voice disagreements without fear of them escalating into an argument. If you can't express yourself openly in a friendship, it's not a healthy relationship.

4. **Balancing Give and Take:** Every relationship involves an aspect of give and take. You give your friends time and energy; they give some in return. You share your secrets with them, and they do the same. You prioritize seeing them, and they return the favor. That's just how a friendship works. But the give-and-take aspect of the friendship must be balanced. If it's one-sided, where one person gives more than the other, the friendship is unlikely to last.

5. **Celebrating Each Other's Successes:** In a healthy relationship, you celebrate each other's successes. If your friend makes the sports team, you should be happy for them, even if you didn't make the cut. While it's natural to feel disappointed if your friends achieve something you haven't, it's important to put those feelings aside and celebrate their successes. And remember, they should also do the same for you.

6. **Taking Interest in Each Other's Lives:** For a friendship to be strong, it's important to be actively involved in each other's lives. This means taking an interest in their hobbies, showing your support, and checking in on them regularly. If your friends

aren't interested in your life, how will they know when you face challenges?

7. **Being There for Each Other:** True friends are there for you when you need them. Whether you need a good chat, a fun distraction, or just want to hang out, having friends there for you shows their reliability and trustworthiness. It doesn't mean you have to drop everything to support them. For example, it doesn't make you a bad friend if you're swamped with exams and can't visit them. The key is to support them when they need you and know they will do the same for you.

While these are all signs of a strong friendship, there are also some warning signs, or "red flags," to look out for. These signs might indicate that a friendship is unhealthy.

Red Flags in Unhealthy Friendships

Unfortunately, not all friendships are healthy. Even when you and your friends are good people, sometimes a friendship just isn't meant to be. Sticking around in an unhealthy friendship can be harmful, so it's important to recognize when to let go of a friendship that's no longer good for you.

But how can you spot when a friendship is turning sour? Here are some warning signs to look out for.

1. **Constant Negativity:** If a friend always sees the downside of a situation, that negativity may also affect you. Everyone has off days and tough times, but looking for positives in life is important.

   If your friends are always negative, you may lose sight of all the great things around you. This could end up bringing you down. Try to surround yourself with people who brighten your day, not darken it.

2. **Lack of Respect:** Respect is key in any friendship. Without respect, there's no trust. If your friend doesn't respect you, they might not consider your feelings or needs. This could lead to drama and heartache.

   Suppose you notice that your friends don't respect you, or they don't show you the respect you deserve. In that case, you should take it as a warning sign and consider whether these are friendships worth sticking with.

3. **Control Issues:** If a friend tries to control your choices — like what you wear, where you go, or what you say — it's a significant red flag.

   It's okay for a friend to offer advice; some friends naturally like to plan things more than others. Still, your friends should always respect your individuality and opinions. If a friend tries to control you and doesn't let you be you, they might not truly appreciate you.

4. **Imbalance of Give and Take:** A healthy friendship is built on a balance of give and take. If there's an imbalance, it's usually a warning sign that something isn't right. If your friend doesn't offer you support in the same way you support them, or only reaches out when they need something, that's a sign of imbalance.

   If you can't rely on your friends when you need them, or if you're always making sacrifices and they're not doing the same for you, it's a red flag in the friendship.

5. **Jealousy:** Jealousy can be damaging in friendships. If your friends are jealous of your success or something you have accomplished, it shows they aren't truly happy for you.

   Jealousy can be destructive in friendships, so if you notice this trait, you may need to reconsider the health of the relationship.

6. **Constant Criticism:** If you always feel you are being criticized or judged by your friends, it can be hard to be yourself around them. For example, if your friends are critical of how you dress, your hobbies, what you eat, or how you talk, you might feel like they don't appreciate you.

   Of course, everyone is entitled to their own opinions, but constant criticism is hurtful and unpleasant. If this happens, it might be a sign you're in an unhealthy friendship.

Recognizing and acknowledging red flags in a friendship can be challenging and emotional, but it's important for your well-being. It's normal to feel sad or conflicted about letting go of a friendship, even if it's unhealthy. Ending a friendship or distancing yourself from an unhealthy friend is never easy, but remember that you deserve to be surrounded by people who uplift and respect you.

Now that you know how to distinguish between healthy and unhealthy friendships, it's time to put that knowledge to use. Below, you'll find a case study with questions to help you identify the features of an unhealthy friendship. You can also complete a friendship checkup to assess the state of your friendships and identify any warning signs you should address. Let's get started!

Isabella, Ava, and Zoe

Isabella, Ava, and Zoe were inseparable at the start of the school year. They shared a lot of fun times together, but after a while, Isabella started feeling left out. Ava and Zoe sometimes whispered and excluded her from their conversations, making her feel uncomfortable and anxious. Eventually, she spoke to her older sister about it, who helped her recognize the unhealthy elements in her friendship with Ava and Zoe. Isabella then made the brave decision to distance herself from Ava and Zoe. She started spending more time with other friends who included her in everything and treated her with kindness and respect. This tough decision led her towards healthier friendships where she felt happy and valued.

Answer the following questions about Isabella, Ava, and Zoe.

1. **Can you identify the signs of an unhealthy friendship in the story of Isabella, Ava, and Zoe?**

   Ava + Zoe left

   isabella out.

2. **How did Isabella handle the situation when she realized her friends weren't treating her well?**

   She told someone

   She trusted!

3. **What would you do if you were in Isabella's position?**

   Same

4. **What do you look for in new friends? What are the most important qualities?**

   Kind, loving faith, truth

Activity: Friendship Check-Up

You probably have some awesome friends you enjoy spending time with who support you and make you feel great. But you may also have other friends you're not quite sure about. Perhaps you can't pinpoint what it is, but something doesn't feel right. That's where this exercise comes in. In this activity, you'll answer a few simple questions about your friends to determine whether your friendships are on the right track.

Carefully consider each question before deciding whether you agree or not. Once you've completed the table, write a short summary of how you feel about this friendship. Is it good for you, or not so much? What are you going to do about it? Remember, it can be tough to let go of friendships, but sometimes it's the best thing for you.

Friendship Audit With [   ]

	AGREE	NEUTRAL	DISAGREE
I feel like I can be myself around my friend.	☺	😐	☹
My friend accepts me for who I am.	☺	😐	☹
I can count on my friend when I need them.	☺	😐	☹
My friend doesn't criticize me or make me feel self-conscious.	☺	😐	☹
I can trust my friend with all my secrets.	☺	😐	☹
My friend makes me feel special/valuable.	☺	😐	☹
I can express my opinions around my friend.	☺	😐	☹
I feel like I take just as much as I give in the friendship.	☺	😐	☹
My friend treats me with kindness and respect.	☺	😐	☹
My friend is never jealous of my success.	☺	😐	☹

If most of your answers (5 or more out of 10) are "neutral" or "disagree," there might be some issues in your friendship, and it might be time to reassess.

Review:

Key Takeaways

A healthy friendship is one where you feel loved, valued, and supported and can be yourself no matter what. Keep an eye out for warning signs, like jealousy, control issues, or lack of respect. These might indicate that you are in an unhealthy relationship.

OVERCOMING FRIENDSHIP
CHALLENGES

Whether in a healthy friendship or facing some challenges, hitting a few bumps along the way is normal. Disagreements are a natural part of being friends, especially when you and your friends have different personalities. But don't worry—challenges like these are completely normal in any friendship. What's most important is knowing how to navigate and resolve any problems so that you can keep enjoying each other's company and have fun together.

In this chapter, we'll explore conflict and uncover why it might arise between you and your friends. We'll unlock the secrets of making up after disagreements and discover ways to handle tricky feelings like jealousy. At the end of the chapter, you can use the skills you've learned in a case study and role-play exercise. Ready to dive in?

Understanding Conflict

Conflict sounds like a scary word, but everyone deals with it—at school, at home, and even on sports teams. It's when you and someone else can't agree, leading to an argument. Some people confuse conflict with fighting. While they have similar traits, they are not quite the same. Conflict is a disagreement or dispute, while fighting involves hostile behavior, often accompanied by anger or aggression.

While disagreements aren't nice, they're not always bad. Sometimes, it's good to clear the air. In fact, working through an argument can make friendships stronger. Let's look at some common causes of friction in a friendship:

CONFLICT

CAUSES

1. Misunderstanding
2. Jealousy
3. Diverging Interests
4. Different Values / Beliefs
5. Peer Pressure
6. Feeling Left Out

RESOLUTION

1. Active Listening
2. "I" Statements
3. Fair Communication
4. Finding A Compromise
5. Apologizing When Necessary

1. **Misunderstanding** — Little mix-ups can happen between friends. Maybe you misunderstood a joke, or perhaps you both got confused about plans for hanging out. These misunderstandings can lead to frustration but can often be resolved by talking it out.

2. **Jealousy** — Sometimes, if a friend has something you wish you had or they achieved something you wanted to, it might make you feel jealous. This is a natural feeling, but it can sometimes lead to negative feelings in a friendship if not handled with care.

3. **Diverging Interests** — As you grow up, your interests will naturally change, and you may enjoy doing different things. For example, you and your friend might have loved playing games together, but what if one of you now wants to hang out at the mall instead? This can lead to feelings of being left out.

4. **Different Values or Beliefs** — As you get older, you may develop different opinions or values from your friends. These differences can sometimes lead to disagreements.

5. **Peer Pressure** — Sometimes, friends might pressure you to do things you don't want to do. This pressure can cause stress, leading to disagreements or hurt feelings between friends.

6. **Feeling Left Out** — Feeling left out is a big deal in friendships. If a friend feels ignored or less important than others in a group, it can lead to sadness and tension in the friendship.

Remember that friendships go through ups and downs, and conflicts are a natural part of that journey. The key to maintaining strong friendships is not avoiding them but learning how to handle them with care, empathy, and open communication. That way, you can keep your friendships strong, even as you grow and change!

Let's look at how to manage and resolve disagreements.

Conflict Resolution Techniques

While conflict is normal in any friendship, it is important that you know how to resolve it effectively, without hurting your friends or them hurting you. Resolving disputes is an important life skill. The sooner you learn it, the better. Here are five conflict resolution techniques to try when you argue with a friend.

1. Active Listening

Active listening means allowing the other person to talk and paying attention to what they are saying. Sometimes, we get so caught up with how we will respond to their words that we don't really hear what our friends are trying to tell us. This can make the argument even worse. When you're in an argument, focus on your friend's words and feelings before responding.

2. Using "I" Statements

It's easy to play the "blame game" when involved in a conflict, but blaming a friend won't resolve the hard feelings, and can worsen things. Instead of blaming them for everything, focus on using "I" statements. For example, instead of saying, "You don't pay attention to me anymore," say, "I feel like we don't spend enough time together, which hurts my feelings." "I" statements help you communicate your feelings without blaming others.

3. Fair Communication

If you're in a disagreement with a friend, stick to what you're really arguing about. Avoid digging up past issues, as it will only draw the conflict out and prevent the issue from being resolved. For instance, if you feel left out, concentrate on discussing that. Don't bring up other issues, like jealousy, as the argument will only escalate, and you'll unlikely resolve the problem.

4. Finding a Compromise

The goal of conflict resolution is to find a compromise. A compromise is when you both agree on something fair. It usually involves a bit of give and take. If you actively listen to your friend and focus on the issue, you should be able to find a middle ground for any problem. For example, if you feel your friend is leaving you out, perhaps you could agree to hang out together on Friday afternoons, leaving Saturdays for her to spend time with her other friends. You may not always get everything you want when finding a middle ground, but the important thing is you both feel heard, cared for, and satisfied with the result.

5. Apologizing When Necessary

Saying sorry can be tough, especially if you feel it's not your fault. But knowing when to apologize and making the effort to do so is crucial for keeping your friendships healthy. If you know you made a mistake, it's important to apologize. It can help clear the air and get things back on track.

Conflict can happen for lots of different reasons. Knowing how to talk it out and make up with a friend can keep your friendships happy and strong.

So, how do you deal with jealousy in a friendship?

Dealing With Jealousy

Jealousy can be a tricky emotion, but it's one that everyone experiences from time to time. It's that feeling you get when your friend has something you want, or maybe they're getting more attention than you.

Feeling jealous of someone with more friends or better things than you is natural, but acting on those feelings won't change anything.

Instead, it might hurt your friendship and make your friend feel bad, leading to problems. Here are some reasons you might feel jealous:

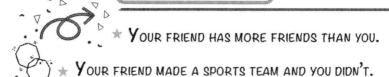

CAUSES OF JEALOUSY

★ YOUR FRIEND HAS MORE FRIENDS THAN YOU.

★ YOUR FRIEND MADE A SPORTS TEAM AND YOU DIDN'T.

★ YOUR FRIEND HAS SOMETHING COOL THAT YOU WANT, LIKE A NEW PHONE.

★ YOUR FRIEND HAS A BOYFRIEND AND YOU DON'T.

Remember, it's normal to feel jealous sometimes, but acting mean or unkind because of it isn't fair to your friend. They haven't done anything wrong.

If you feel jealous of your friend, it's important that you focus on discovering the root of the jealousy. Here are some ways to deal with jealousy, so it doesn't cause problems in your friendships:

WAYS TO DEAL WITH JEALOUSY

* ASK YOURSELF, "WHY AM I JEALOUS OF MY FRIEND?"

* TALK TO YOUR FRIEND ABOUT YOUR FEELINGS AND EXPLAIN WHY YOU FEEL THAT WAY.

* THINK ABOUT HOW YOUR JEALOUSY MIGHT HAVE AFFECTED YOUR FRIEND'S FEELINGS.

* FOCUS ON IMPROVING YOURSELF INSTEAD OF COMPARING YOURSELF TO YOUR FRIENDS.
  For example, if your friend made a sports team and you didn't, practice more, be dedicated, and try again next time.

Another common cause of conflict in a friendship is diverging interests. This happens when you and your friend start to like different things. It's not about someone being mean or doing anything wrong; it's just a natural part of growing up. But if it's not handled carefully, it can strain a friendship.

How do you manage this?

Diverging Interests

As you get older, your interests might change, and that's totally normal. You might find that you and your friends no longer like the same things. While this can cause tension in your friendships, it doesn't mean you can't still be friends. Here's how to manage diverging interests and keep your friendships strong:

- **Accept That Change is Normal**: It's okay if you and your friends start liking different things. Everyone has unique interests.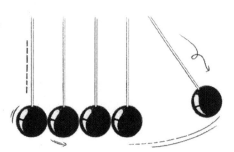

- **Give Space and Support**: Allow your friends to pursue their interests, and ask for the same space in return. Support each other's individual passions.

- **Find Common Ground**: Look for activities or interests you still enjoy together, like shopping or watching movies.

- **Respect Individual Interests**: Understand that having different interests is okay, and focus on what you still have in common.

- **Make New Friends**: If your friend has a new interest you're not into, it's an opportunity for both of you to make new friends who share these new interests. This doesn't mean you're replacing each other; you're just expanding your friendship circles.

Remember, it's normal for friends to develop different interests as they grow up. What's most important is how you handle it. With understanding and communication, your friendship can still be strong and fun, even if you like different things.

Now that you have learned what conflict is, what causes conflict, and how to navigate conflict in your friendship, it's time to put that knowledge to the test. Below is a case study with some questions about how to handle conflict. You will also find a role-play activity where you can practice the conflict resolution techniques learned in this chapter. Good luck!

Olivia and Sophie

Since kindergarten, Sophie and Olivia have been best friends, sharing everything from secrets to hobbies. But when Sophie started taking dance classes, she soon made a new friend, Mandy. Since Mandy was also in their school, Sophie started spending more time with Mandy and less with Olivia.

Olivia started feeling that Sophie was ignoring her for her new friend, leading to her feeling left out. However, after taking some time apart, they decided to talk about the issue openly. Olivia expressed her feelings of being left out, and Sophie apologized, explaining that she didn't intend to hurt Olivia.

After explaining how they both felt, the girls agreed to be more considerate of each other's feelings in the future. Olivia tried to understand Sophie's new interests, even attending a dance class or two. This not only strengthened her bond with Sophie, but allowed her to become friends with Mandy, as well.

Answer the following questions about Olivia and Sophie.

1. How did Olivia and Sophie sort things out?

_____

_____

_____

2. What strategies did Olivia and Sophie use to communicate their feelings effectively? (Hint: Consider how they expressed their emotions and listened to each other.)

_____

_____

_____

3. How can you apply these conflict resolution techniques in your own friendships?

_____

_____

_____

Activity: Conflict Resolution Role-Play

In this activity, you will explore three scenarios involving conflicts between friends. Your task is to apply the conflict resolution techniques you've learned in this chapter to address the issues in each situation. Write down the strategies and steps you would take, or role-play the scenarios with a friend or family member to practice in real time. Reflect on what you have done and learned after each scenario.

Scenario 1: Amy and Stephanie

Amy and Stephanie have to work together on a school project. They aren't really friends, and soon run into trouble with the project. While Amy wants to work together to complete the project, Stephanie isn't interested in working on the project. She assumes Amy will do all the work.

How should Amy broach the topic with Stephanie so they can work together on this project?

- Consider Amy's feelings and how she can communicate them to Stephanie.

- Think about how Stephanie might respond and how Amy can encourage teamwork.

Teach Stephanie the consept!

Scenario 2: Elsa and Liza

Elsa and Liza have been best friends for years, but after both girls tried out for the school soccer team, Liza was chosen for the team, while Elsa was not. This made Elsa feel jealous of Liza. As a result, she started acting differently toward Liza, hurting her feelings.

How can Liza and Elsa work together to resolve this conflict and remain friends?

- Reflect on the emotions involved and how open communication can alleviate the issue.

- Consider ways they can support each other, even though their circumstances have changed.

Scenario 3: Merida and Odette

Merida and Odette have always been best friends. They had the same interests and dreamed of becoming professional dancers. However, when they went to high school, Merida started taking acting classes while Odette continued dancing. They started drifting apart, and Odette felt Merida was neglecting her to pursue new hobbies.

What can Merida and Odette do to preserve their friendship while giving each other space to grow?

- Think about the importance of understanding and respecting each other's evolving interests.

- Consider strategies to reconnect and find shared activities or interests.

Key Takeaways

As friendships evolve and interests change, conflicts may naturally arise. Navigating these challenges is crucial for maintaining strong, resilient friendships. Actively listening to your friends, using "I" statements, emphasizing fair communication, finding a compromise, and apologizing when necessary are just some of the ways to resolve disputes with your friends and keep your friendships strong.

LOSING FRIENDS AND MOVING ON

Losing a friend is not something anyone wants to experience. It can be painful, especially if you lose your best friend. But as tough as it is, losing friends is just something that happens as you get older. When you're younger, you might have lots of friends, but as you grow up and your interests change, you may naturally drift apart from some friends. It's not fun, but it's a normal part of life. The good news is that even if you lose some old friends, you'll make plenty of new ones as you grow older!

There are many reasons why friends might drift apart, and it's totally normal to feel a bit sad or confused about it. But there are ways to help you feel better and understand what's happening. It may not be the most fun thing to think about, but learning how to handle these feelings can turn something negative into a positive experience.

In this chapter, we'll explore why friends sometimes grow apart, and how to cope with the feelings that come with it. We'll give you some helpful strategies for dealing with these changes, so you can bounce back and feel great. Later, you'll get to use your knowledge in a case study about two friends who drifted apart, and try an activity that lets you explore your own thoughts about friendships.

Let's dive in and discover why these changes happen as we grow up, and how to handle them.

Reasons For Losing Friends

Have you ever heard the saying, "Life happens?" It's an old saying, but it's still true. Sometimes, no matter how hard we try or how much we care, we drift apart from a friend. It's a normal part of growing up, even though it's tough.

You may wonder why people lose friends in the first place. While there are many reasons for losing friends and breaking up friendships, here are five of the most common ones:

1. Changing Schools

Sometimes, friends drift apart when they go to different schools. When you leave elementary school, you might go to the same middle or high school as some of your friends, but other friends might go somewhere else. Whether that school is near or far, you could drift apart from the friends who aren't at your school.

Even if you try hard to stay close, it's tough to keep a friendship going when you're not in the same place daily. You're at school a lot, so you won't see friends from other schools as often. If you don't do the same after-school activities, you might not see them much at all.

It's sad to drift apart from friends just because you attend different schools, but it's natural. Once you get used to your new school, you'll make new friends, and your old friends might drift further away. That doesn't mean you can't stay friends if you're at different schools, but it might take more effort.

If you stop being friends because you or your friend changed schools, it's usually not anybody's fault. It's just a friendship that has run its course. You can always look back on the good times you had together and remember them with a smile.

2. Moving Away

Moving to a new place can be hard on friendships, just like changing schools. If you move to a different town, or even a different state or country, it can make it difficult to maintain friendships. You won't see your friends as often, and talking to them might be tricky if there's a time difference.

But don't worry, moving away doesn't mean you have to stop being friends. It's okay if you drift apart a little — it doesn't mean you did anything wrong or that your friendship was bad. Losing touch with friends sometimes is a normal part of growing up, and it can happen to anyone.

If you want to stay close to your friends after moving, you'll just have to try a bit harder to stay in touch.

3. Disagreements

Sometimes friendships end because of disagreements. While we discussed conflict resolution earlier in the book, some problems simply can't be fixed. When that happens, it might mean saying goodbye to a friendship. Ending a friendship over a disagreement is sad, and you might feel different emotions.

You should always try to work things out, but sometimes, it's just not possible. Maybe you both feel strongly about something, or neither wants to give in. That could mean the end of your friendship.

Even if an argument ends a friendship, it doesn't mean you have to be mad at your friend forever. Holding on to anger might make you forget all the fun times you had together, and leave you feeling upset. It's really important to understand how you feel about a friendship ending, no matter why it happened, so you can feel better and make new friends.

4. Diverging Interests

Another common reason friendships sometimes end is when you and your friend start to like different things. We have discussed this several times before, but diverging interests can cause friends to drift apart. As you grow up, you might find new hobbies or interests. Maybe you stop taking dance lessons or are no longer interested in swimming or collecting stickers.

If those shared activities were a big part of your friendship, growing apart can be tough. But it's okay if your interests change; that's just part of getting older.

If a friendship ends because you both like different things now, it doesn't mean you did anything wrong. Sometimes, friendships just naturally come to an end. You'll discover new hobbies and make new friends who enjoy the same things. Your old friend will do the same.

And remember, even if you don't share the same hobbies anymore, you can still be nice to each other. You'll always have the fun memories you shared when you liked the same things.

5. Unhealthy Friendships

You might remember learning about healthy and unhealthy friendships earlier in this book. Recognizing an unhealthy friendship is really important, and sometimes the best thing you can do for yourself and your friend is to end the friendship.

If you feel like you're not being treated with respect, support, or kindness, it might be time to look for friends who will treat you right. Trust is crucial, too. If you can't trust each other, it might be best to move on.

Ending an unhealthy friendship is a big decision and can be really sad, but it doesn't mean you did something wrong. In fact, it shows that you're wise enough to know when a situation isn't good for you and brave enough to do what's best for you and your friend.

It's normal to feel a mix of emotions when a friendship ends, no matter the reason. You might feel sad, confused, or even relieved, and that's okay. Healthily handling those feelings is a big part of growing up, and it helps you learn how to be a good friend in the future. Remember, you're learning and growing, and caring for yourself is important.

Dealing With the Loss of a Friend

Losing a friend can be tough, and it's normal to feel different emotions. You might feel sad one minute, angry the next, or even lost. It's okay to feel that way. Your feelings are normal, and you don't need to be embarrassed or ashamed.

However, it is important to process the feelings of losing a friend. If you don't process and overcome these feelings, they can have lasting impacts and may affect how you treat friends in the future.

Why It's Okay to Feel Sad When You Lose a Friend

It's natural to feel many different emotions when you lose a friend. You might feel angry or wish you could just forget about them. It's also totally okay to feel sad about it.

Even if you had a fight or didn't always get along, you were still friends. That friendship was special, and it's normal to miss it. You might feel a little lost or unsure about what to do next, and that's all right. Your feelings are real. It's important to recognize them and it's also essential to figure out healthy ways to handle those feelings.

Remembering the fun times and why you became friends in the first place can help. Think about the laughs, the shared secrets, and the great times you had together. Focusing on those happy memories can make the sadness a bit easier to handle.

Let's look at some other ways to process losing a friend.

Coping Strategies After Losing a Friend

Losing a friend can be really hard, but there are healthy ways to handle all the feelings you might have. Here are some strategies that can help you process your feelings, focus on the good times, and feel better:

1. Giving Yourself Time

Healing takes time, and feeling sad or confused is okay. Give yourself time to process your feelings, and remember that those feelings will ease as you move forward.

2. Seeking Support

Seeking support from your friends and family can help you process the feelings of losing a friend. Talking to them can make you feel loved and cherished. No matter what, they're there for you, ready to listen and remind you that you're not alone.

3. Channeling Negative Emotions into Positive Actions

Turn your negative feelings into something positive, like exercising, journaling, or painting. Doing so can help release negative emotions and create something beautiful in the process. It's like giving those sad or angry feelings a new, happier home.

4. Seeking Healthy Outlets

You might want to write about your feelings instead of talking about them. That's okay! Journaling, meditating, or chatting with other friends can help. Even if you don't show your writing to anyone, getting those feelings out can help you understand them and make you feel much better.

5. Staying Positive

Instead of focusing on the negative aspects of a relationship, focus on the good memories and what you've learned from the experience. This can help you cherish the good times you spent together and keep a positive outlook for the future.

6. Seeking Professional Help

If those feelings just won't go away, or you're having a really tough time, it's okay to ask for help from a counselor or therapist. These experts know all about feelings and can help you find new ways to cope.

7. Joining Clubs or Groups

Finding a club or group that shares your interests can help you make new friends and keep busy. It can be a fun way to move on and find joy in activities you love.

Remember, it's okay to feel sad and emotional when losing a friend, and various coping strategies can serve as tools to help navigate those feelings. Experimenting with these tools lets you find what works best for you. With time and effort, the difficult emotions will begin to ease. Remember, you have the strength to get through this.

Ava and Lucy

Ava and Lucy were like two peas in a pod since kindergarten. They laughed together, shared secrets, and even had matching friendship bracelets. Growing up, they created loads of fun and unforgettable memories.

But then, something big happened. When they turned 12, Lucy's family decided to move to another city. Both girls promised to write letters, call each other, and remain best friends forever, but as time went on, things began to change.

They started to make new friends in their own cities, and their interests started to go in different directions. They tried hard to keep in touch, but the distance made things tricky. Ava missed Lucy a lot and felt really sad at first.

But then, Ava realized that it was normal to feel this way. She thought about all the good times she and Lucy had shared and smiled. She started to make new friends and found joy in new hobbies. Even though she missed Lucy, she knew their memories would always be a special part of her life.

This story shows that it's normal for friendships to change and that feeling sad about it is okay. It also teaches us to learn from these experiences, make new friends, and keep happy memories in our hearts.

Answer the following questions about Lucy and Ava.

1. **Why did Ava and Lucy's friendship drift apart?**

....

....

....

2. **How did Ava cope with losing her close friendship with Lucy?**

....

....

....

3. **Can you think of strategies Ava used that might help you if you lose a friend?**

....

....

....

Activity: Letter to a Friend

Sometimes, writing down our feelings can help when we're sad or confused. In this exercise, you'll have the chance to write a letter to a friend you may have lost touch with or grown apart from. Don't worry, you won't actually send the letter, so you can be completely honest about your feelings.

You might find that writing this letter brings up strong emotions, and that's totally normal. If anything becomes too much, please don't hesitate to talk to an adult you trust. They can help you understand what you're feeling.

Take your time, and write whatever feels right for you. Here are some questions that might help guide your thoughts:

- What do you miss most about your friend?

- Are there things you wish you could have done differently?

- What happy memories do you still hold close?

- How have you grown or changed since your friendship changed?

- Is there anything you'd want to tell them if they were right in front of you now?

Remember, this letter is just for you. It's a safe space to explore your feelings, and there's no right or wrong way to do it. Take as long as you need, and be kind to yourself. You're doing great!

Here's a little prompt to help you get started:

Dear _____

I've been thinking a lot about our friendship and all the fun times we used to have. Lately, things have changed, and I miss how close we used to be. I wanted to write you this letter to tell you...

Key Takeaways

Losing a friend is never easy, but it is a normal part of growing up. Moving, changing schools, diverging interests, and arguments may cause a friendship to end. It's okay to feel sad when a friendship ends. However, developing the right coping techniques to deal with these emotions is important. Seeking support, remembering the past, channeling negative thoughts into positive actions, and seeking professional help are ways to process losing a friend or friendship.

BULLYING AND PEER PRESSURE

As great as they are, friendships can sometimes be challenged by bullying and peer pressure. These aren't minor issues — they are serious problems that deserve attention, even when they involve close friends. Bullying can stir up negative feelings, shaking your self-confidence. Meanwhile, peer pressure can push you to act in ways you're uncomfortable with, even doing things against your principles and beliefs.

Learning to recognize bullying and peer pressure is crucial. As you enter your teenage years, the nature of bullying will change, and peer pressure often becomes more complex. Since they can harm your happiness and well-being, knowing how to spot them and what to do when they creep into your friendships is vital.

In this chapter, we will uncover the signs of bullying and peer pressure and learn some effective strategies to tackle them. You'll also read a case study and several scenarios that show how peer pressure and bullying can appear in friendships, giving you a chance to apply what you've learned. But before we jump into the exercises, let's take a moment to understand bullying.

Bullying

Being bullied or bullying others is never acceptable. There's a massive gap between light-hearted teasing and joking among friends and bullying. Just because someone is your friend doesn't give them the right to bully you or for you to bully them.

Let's delve into what bullying truly means and how it's different from simple, friendly teasing.

Understanding Bullying

The Anti-Bullying Alliance defines bullying as "the repetitive, intentional hurting of one person or group by another person or group, where the relationship involves an imbalance of power" (n.d.). Put simply, bullying is when someone repeatedly hurts or upsets another person on purpose, taking advantage of a situation where they have more power or control. This behavior is always unacceptable.

When you're younger, you might have disagreements with your friends over small things, like which toy to play with, where to sit, or which snack to eat. However, when these disagreements escalate to name-calling or making fun of others, it becomes a type of bullying.

No one should have to endure bullying. Sadly, bullies can be found in most schools. But, identifying bullying is not always easy with all the different types. It becomes even more challenging when those involved are friends.

So, what exactly are the different forms of bullying?

Different Kinds of Bullying

Bullying takes many shapes and forms.

- **Physical Bullying**

  You might first think of bullying as pushing, hitting, or physically hurting someone else. This is known as physical bullying. It's just as serious as other types of bullying and is usually easier to spot.

- **Verbal Bullying**

  There's also verbal bullying. This happens when someone calls another person names, teases them, or spreads rumors about them. Verbal bullying often happens in the open, where many people can see or hear it. This can sometimes lead to an escalation in the bullying, where more people join in as the name-calling and rumors spread.

- **Cyberbullying**

  A type of bullying that's become more common with teenagers is cyberbullying. This is like verbal bullying, but it happens online or over social media. Because social media posts can be seen by so many people, this kind of bullying can spread fast and far. Posting embarrassing pictures of someone without their consent is also considered cyberbullying.

Each of these types of bullying is harmful and mean. If someone intentionally hurts another person without feeling sorry, they are a bully. Being a bully isn't a good thing, and you should look out for it in school and at home. But where does the boundary lie between friendly teasing and bullying?

The Difference Between Friendly Teasing and Bullying

Teasing can be a light-hearted way for friends to interact with each other. For example, if you have a fun nickname for your friend and they're okay with it, it's usually seen as friendly banter. Similarly, if your friends gently tease you about harmless subjects, like a crush you have, this isn't usually considered bullying.

These are examples of friendly teasing. So, what's the difference between friendly teasing and bullying? It comes down to why the teasing is happening and how it makes the other person feel. Friendly teasing comes from a place of love, laughter, and fun, whereas bullying results in tears and hurt feelings.

So, it usually isn't bullying if you don't feel hurt by your friends' jokes or actions. But situations and emotions change. If the same fun nickname you give your friend is used negatively or starts to make them feel bad, it's shifted into bullying territory.

Take a moment to consider how your words and actions might make the other person feel. This awareness can help you determine if your teasing is fun or might be causing unintentional harm.

STRATEGIES TO HANDLE BULLYING

Bullying is never okay, and it's important to know how to handle it if you or a friend is being bullied. Here are four strategies that might help:

1. STANDING UP FOR YOURSELF

Bullies usually don't like it when someone stands up to them. If you let them know that what they're doing isn't okay, they might stop. This might be tough, especially if it's your friends who are the bullies, but you have the right to tell them they're wrong.

2. GETTING HELP

If standing up to the bullies doesn't work, it's really important to talk to an adult you trust, such as a parent, teacher, or coach. They can offer help and advice on how to deal with the situation.

3. STAYING POSITIVE

Bullying can really hurt your self-esteem, but remember, you're not the one with the problem—the bully is. Try to keep your confidence high, and don't let their mean words affect how you feel about yourself.

4. HELPING OTHERS

If you see someone else being bullied, you can make a big difference by standing up for them. Knowing someone cares can be a huge help to a person who's being bullied. Even if you're not the one being bullied, you can help put a stop to it.

Remember, no one deserves to be bullied, and it's never okay to bully others. It's okay to joke with friends, but not if it hurts their feelings. If you're unsure, it's always best to check in with your friends and ensure they're okay with the joke or teasing.

Peer Pressure

As you grow up and enter your teen years, you might face peer pressure. Wanting to fit in and being scared of being left out can make you more likely to feel peer pressure. Sometimes, peer pressure can lead to bad or unsafe situations. That's why it's important for you, as a tween, to understand peer pressure and how to deal with it.

Understanding Peer Pressure

Peer pressure happens when your friends or group influence your choices or actions. It's like when your friends nudge or sway you to behave a certain way. Peer pressure can be positive. For example, your friends might encourage you to try harder on your homework or to put more effort into activities you enjoy.

But peer pressure isn't always good. It can sometimes be negative. This kind of peer pressure might push you to do things you don't really want to do, or that go against what you believe is right. For example, your friends might try convincing you to get a piercing, even when you don't want one. They might even encourage you to act in mean ways towards other people, which could turn you into a bully.

Peer pressure usually happens gradually, where you adjust your behavior bit by bit to feel more accepted by your friends. This typically happens when you become a teenager because fitting in with your friends can feel important.

Fear that your friends will reject you if you don't follow their lead is a big reason why peer pressure happens. When peer pressure is about good things, like studying more or helping others, it's not a problem. But, peer pressure can become a problem when it pushes you to do things that aren't good for you or make you uncomfortable. So, what should you do when you start to notice peer pressure?

Dealing with peer pressure from your friends can be hard, and you might feel worried about them rejecting or not liking you anymore. But remember, it's important that your friends respect your choices—and you should respect yourself, too.

Here are four tips that can help you handle peer pressure when you notice it:

Confident Communication

Talking confidently and assertively with your friends is a really important life skill. If there's something you don't want to do, tell your friends in a clear way that shows them you're not comfortable with it, and that you won't change your mind. For instance, if your friends are trying to convince you to get a piercing, but you don't want one, you can say, "No, I really don't want to get a piercing today.".

Decision Making Skills

Being able to make good decisions, even when you feel under pressure, is another important skill. If something doesn't feel right to you, or you're uncomfortable, you should think about what the right thing to do is and tell your friends what you've decided. Remember, it's okay to say, "No."

Know Your Values

If you believe in your own values and beliefs, it'll be easier to stand up to your friends when you're uncomfortable with something. If you believe that what you're doing is right, you shouldn't feel embarrassed to do it. If your friends really respect you, they'll understand and respect your values.

Ask For Help

If you find it hard to stand up for yourself, it might be a good idea to talk to an adult or mentor. They can help you resist the urge to give into negative peer pressure and can give you some really good advice on how to handle the situation.

Now that you know how to spot and handle bullying and peer pressure, it's time to put that knowledge into action. You'll go through a case study and work through several scenarios with examples of peer pressure and bullying. This way, you can practice the strategies you've just learned. Good luck!

Michelle and Jade

Michelle and Jade were good friends, but things changed when Michelle was chosen for the school's soccer team, and Jade was not. Jade started spreading unkind rumors about Michelle and bullying her at school, even in front of other students. This made Michelle really sad and confused about why Jade was so mean. She knew that Jade's actions were wrong.

Michelle decided to talk to her parents, teachers, and other friends about what was happening. They gave her a lot of support and advice. Taking their advice, Michelle distanced herself from Jade to protect herself from more bullying. Michelle also saw how her friends stood up for her, telling others that Jade's rumors were untrue and that it wasn't right for Jade to treat Michelle this way.

Later, Jade realized what she had done. She understood that she had been influenced by her other friends to bully Michelle and spread unkind rumors because she was upset about the soccer team. Jade knew that Michelle hadn't done anything wrong, and that it wasn't fair to treat her that way. She apologized to Michelle and their friends, and told everyone that the rumors she had spread weren't true. Michelle accepted Jade's apology, understanding that Jade had been influenced by her other friends, and they became friends again.

Answer the following questions about Jade and Michelle.

1. How did Michelle handle the situation when Jade started bullying her?

_____

_____

_____

2. What role did Michelle's other friends play?

_____

_____

3. Can you think of a time when you've faced peer pressure or bullying? What did you do to handle the situation?

_____

_____

_____

Activity: What Would You Do?

You'll find instances of bullying or peer pressure instances in the three scenarios below. After reading the scenario carefully, consider how to use the skills you've learned in this chapter to handle these real-life situations. Write down your actions and what you would say to help resolve the situation and support those involved.

Scenario 1: Becca's Photo

Becca is a classmate of yours. She's not part of the popular group and often gets teased or bullied by some of the popular boys and girls. One day, you find out that one of the popular girls has found a really embarrassing photo of Becca from when she was younger. This girl wants to share the photo with everyone in class, including all of Becca's friends, and even the boy she likes.

What actions could you take in this situation to help Becca?

....

....

....

....

....

Scenario 2: The Popularity Contest

There's a popular online game that almost everyone at school is playing. Your friends have all joined and are pressuring you to do the same, even though you're not really interested. They say that everyone who's cool is playing, and you'll be left out if you don't. They're even ranking each other based on their game scores and discussing it at lunch.

What would you do in this situation? How would you handle the peer pressure?

_____

_____

_____

_____

_____

Scenario 3: Magdi's Lunch

Magdi is a student from India attending your school for a semester. Although she's

friendly and intelligent, Magdi doesn't have many friends at school yet. One day, as you and your friends pass by Magdi's lunch table, one of your friends, Kate, starts making fun of Magdi for bringing packed lunch from home instead of buying something from the cafeteria. To make things worse, Kate teases Magdi for bringing a lentil curry to school and says it smells funny.

What would you say to Kate in this situation? Would you stand up for Magdi?

Key Takeaways

As you grow older and become a teenager, you'll likely encounter more instances of peer pressure and bullying. It's important to know how to identify bullying and distinguish it from harmless teasing. In dealing with bullying, standing up for yourself, getting help, staying positive, and understanding the powerful role of helping others can make a big difference.

Peer pressure isn't always a bad thing. Sometimes, it can motivate us to do better. However, negative peer pressure can lead us to behave in ways that aren't true to ourselves or that we're uncomfortable with. Just like with bullying, being assertive, seeking support, holding strong to your values, and making wise decisions can help you navigate the challenges of negative peer pressure.

NAVIGATING FRIENDSHIPS IN AN ONLINE WORLD

The digital world is a big part of our lives and plays an important role in friendships. While you may not make new friends online, your friendships will likely evolve through social media, messaging apps, and other online platforms as you get older. On the one hand, this instant connection is a great way to stay connected, but it can also create some challenges.

This chapter is all about navigating friendships in an online world. We'll uncover the delicate balance of digital communication, ensuring that an emoji isn't misconstrued or a missed chat doesn't lead to feelings of exclusion. By the end, you'll know how to create your own digital safety checklist, ensuring you can safely navigate digital friendships.

Life Before Technology

Before technology, friends kept in touch via letters, waiting weeks or even months to receive a response. Then came the telephone, which offered an instant way to communicate and share news. Fast forward to today, and technology has revolutionized how we communicate with each other. Emails, instant messaging, social media, and video calls allow us to communicate in ways that even 20 years ago seemed impossible.

Let's look at some of the benefits of this instant communication.

1. EXPLORING AND FINDING SHARED INTERESTS ONLINE

2. ONLINE FRIENDS ARE JUST A CLICK AWAY

3. EXPLORING THE WORLD WITH ONLINE FRIENDS

4. STAYING IN TOUCH THROUGH ONLINE FRIENDSHIP

5. PRACTICING COMMUNICATION SKILLS

6. LEARNING TO NAVIGATE THE DIGITAL WORLD

ADVANTAGES ONLINE FRIENDSHIPS

DISADVANTAGES

1. POTENTIAL FOR MISUNDERSTANDINGS

2. WHO'S BEHIND THE SCREEN

3. KEEP YOUR SECRETS SECRET

4. WATCH OUT FOR BULLIES

5. NO YUCKY STUFF

6. YOU'VE GOT A LIFE OUTSIDE THE SCREEN

Benefits of Online & Digital Interactions

Online interactions play an essential role in enhancing and building friendships. Here's why:

1. **Instant Connection:** When life gets hectic, physically spending time with friends can be challenging. Digital platforms provide a solution; you send a message and get a response instantly. This can help maintain a friendship and sense of closeness.

2. **Staying in Touch:** Have you ever had a friend who moved away or switched schools? Beforehand, you might have lost touch with them. But today, you can keep in contact wherever they are.

3. **Sharing Experiences:** Online tools make it easier to share experiences. Whether seeing your friends on holiday, watching a movie together on Zoom, or playing games online. It allows you to share and build a deeper connection.

4. **Practicing Communication Skills**: Chatting online can offer an excellent platform to practice and improve communication skills. For some, sharing feelings and thoughts in writing is easier than talking.

5. **Learning to Navigate the Digital World**: Using online tools responsibly teaches you how to be a good digital citizen. You learn about online etiquette, respectful communication, and the necessity of online safety.

Challenges of Online & Digital Interactions

Maintaining friendships online brings fabulous benefits. However, there are challenges too, and here's what you should keep an eye on:

1. **Potential for Misunderstandings**: Without the benefit of tone or body language, it's easier to get the wrong idea about what someone means in an online chat. It's always good to ask for clarification if you're unsure.

2. **Digital Boldness:** Sometimes, people behave differently when hiding behind a screen. They become bolder and more aggressive, forgetting that their words and actions can negatively affect others.

3. **Who's Behind the Screen**: Sometimes, strangers pretend to be someone they're not when they are online. They might say they're your age when they're really not.

4. **Privacy Concerns**: Don't give out any personal info to people you don't know. Stuff like where you live, your full name, or where you go to school should stay private.

5. **Comparing Yourself to Others:** It's easy to feel like everyone else's life is perfect when scrolling through social media, especially when comparing yourself to influencers. But remember, no one's life is perfect; everyone has challenges.

6. **FOMO (Fear of Missing Out):** Seeing friends share their experiences and activities can lead to feelings of missing out. Particularly if you're not part of the fun.

7. **Digital Distractions:** If you're not careful, the constant ding of messages and notifications can distract you from enjoying real-life experiences and conversations.

8. **Online Bullying:** Sadly, some people use the Internet to be mean to others. If anyone makes you uncomfortable or hurts your feelings, let a trusted adult know immediately.

9. **Inappropriate Stuff**: Let an adult know if an online friend shows you something that feels wrong or icky, like violent images or inappropriate content. You should never be made to feel uncomfortable.

10. **Life Beyond the Screen**: While the digital world is fascinating, nothing can replace face-to-face conversations and real-life experiences. It's essential to find a balance. Remember, there's nothing like stepping away from the screen, breathing in fresh air, and enjoying the world around you!

Remember, the Internet can be a fun place to keep in touch friends and learn new things, but always be careful and let an adult know if something doesn't feel right. Your safety is super important!

Online Friends: The Same Rules Apply

Like friendships in the playground or classroom, online friendships are based on the same principles: respect, trust, empathy, and understanding. The setting might differ — you're communicating through screens rather than face-to-face — but the core values that make a friendship strong remain the same.

The same rules of friendship apply, whether you're chatting online or hanging out together after school. Here's a quick recap of those rules:

1. **Respect**: Always treat others how you want to be treated. Be considerate and kind in your online interactions.

2. **Trust**: Good friends trust each other. When you are online, this means being honest with your friends, keeping promises, and not sharing private conversations or personal information with others.

3. **Empathy**: Understand and respect the feelings of your friends. If they're upset or having a tough day, show them you care and offer your support.

4. **Understanding**: Everyone is unique. Celebrate these differences and try to understand others' viewpoints, even if they don't align with yours.

While these rules of friendship apply universally, the online environment does have certain nuances. As you navigate digital interactions, here are some digital-specific netiquette to keep in mind:

1. **Always Be Polite**: Just because you're online doesn't mean you can forget your manners. Treat your friends the same way you would want to be treated.

2. **Understand That People Are Different**: We all come from different backgrounds and cultures, and sometimes have different opinions. It's okay to disagree with someone, but always do it respectfully.

3. **Be Clear in Your Communications**: Since there's no body language online, ensure your words are clear and not likely to be misunderstood.

4. **Take a Breather**: If someone says something that upsets you, taking a break from the conversation is okay. Take a few deep breaths, think about what you want to say, and return when you're ready.

Now that we've covered online friendship netiquette, let's focus on another crucial aspect — online safety.

Online Safety

Digital interactions with friends can be fun and rewarding! However, just like in the offline world, there are a few things to keep in mind to ensure that everything stays friendly and safe. Think of the Internet like a big city: There are many amazing places to visit and people to meet, but just as you wouldn't share all your secrets with every person you meet in a city, the same goes for online.

- **What to Share and Keep to Yourself**

  When chatting on social media or in open groups, talking about your favorite movies, music, or games is fine. However, be cautious about sharing personal details. Your full name, address, school name, or other identifying information should be kept private. It might be tempting to share more, but remember that not everyone is who they claim to be, and sadly, not everyone has good intentions. Keep your real identity safe and avoid oversharing.

- **Set Your Privacy Settings**

  Privacy settings can help keep your personal data safe. When you're online, adjust your settings to protect information like your location and contact details. Remember, privacy settings ensure only people you trust and know can see your information.

- **Trust Your Gut**

  If something feels off or makes you uncomfortable, trust your instincts. For example, suppose someone is pressuring you to share personal information or send inappropriate messages. In that case, it's okay to end the conversation or block them.

- **Screenshotting and Recording**

  It's essential to respect privacy. Always ask your friends before taking a screenshot or recording a chat. If someone takes one without your permission, it's okay to tell them it's not right and to let a trusted adult know.

- **Handling Bullying or Harassment**

  Unfortunately, cyberbullying is a real issue. Recognize the signs of bullying, such as repeated aggressive messages, spreading rumors, or making threats. Also, remember that it's not your fault if it happens. Report any bullying or harassment to the platform and let a trusted adult know. Remember, no one has the right to make you feel bad or unsafe.

- **Strangers Online**

  Be cautious of friend requests or messages from strangers. While making new friends can be fun, online friendships should be people you already know. Not everyone is who they say they are. However, nice people may seem online; if you don't know them, they are still strangers. Speak to a trusted adult if you're unsure or uneasy about anyone or anything.

- **External Links and Downloads**

  Be careful when clicking on unfamiliar links or downloading files from unknown sources. They could contain viruses or other harmful materials.

- **Create Strong Passwords**

  Protecting your online accounts starts with strong passwords. Use a mix of letters, numbers, and symbols, and avoid using easily guessable information, like your name or birthday. Remember, your password is the first line of defense against someone getting access to your accounts.

Now that you've learned about digital interactions and staying safe online, it's time to put your knowledge to the test. The following case study is about Emma, a young girl who felt down after seeing her friends' seemingly perfect lives on social media. After reading her story, there are some questions for you to answer. Once you've done that, it's time to create a digital safety checklist to help you stay safe online.

Case Study:

Emma

Emma really enjoyed seeing her friends' adventures and hobbies, on social media, especially during holiday breaks from school. But, when she was at home during the holidays, she started to feel sad. It seemed like everyone was leading fun, exciting and happy lives, while she was just at home.

She felt left out and unhappy, wondering why her life wasn't as fun and exciting. She felt worse whenever she saw someone else's happy photos or read about their amazing adventures.

Emma's mom noticed she was upset and talked to her about it. She explained that people often only share their best moments online, creating a "highlight reel." This isn't a complete picture of their lives; everyone has regular days and faces challenges; they just don't usually post those.

After talking with her mom, Emma felt much better. She learned to focus more on enjoying her own experiences rather than comparing her life to the seemingly "perfect" ones she saw online. She understood that everyone has ups and downs, even if they don't share them.

Answer the following questions about Emma's story.

1. Why did Emma feel sad during her holidays?

_____

_____

_____

2. What did Emma's mom explain to her about people's online posts?

_____

_____

_____

3. Why is it important to enjoy your experiences instead of comparing yourself to others' online posts?

_____

_____

_____

Activity: Digital Safety Checklist

Understanding online safety is essential, but putting it into practice is where the real learning begins! In this activity, you will use the knowledge you learned in this chapter to create your digital safety checklist.

Once you've filled this out, take a moment to discuss it with a trusted adult. They might offer some additional insights. Remember, this checklist is to help protect you against online troubles. Keep it handy and stay safe!

MY DIGITAL SAFETY CHECKLIST

Once you've filled this out, take a moment to discuss it with a trusted adult. They might offer some additional insights. Remember, this checklist is to help protect you against online troubles. Keep it handy and stay safe!

WHAT'S A DIGITAL SAFETY CHECKLIST?
It's a personalized guide that helps you make smart choices online. It'll be your go-to handbook, reminding you of safe practices while you are browsing the web, playing games, or chatting with

1. PERSONAL DATA PROTECTION
List down the personal details you believe should never be shared online:

2. PASSWORD SECURITY
Describe how you'll ensure your passwords are difficult to guess, & how often to change them:

3. CLICKING CAUTIOUSLY
When faced with an unfamiliar link, what steps will you take before clicking?

4. COMMUNICATION PROTOCOL
Write down your golden rules about online conversations, including who you will talk to and what things should never be discussed.

5. BALANCING ONLINE AND OFFLINE LIFE
How will you ensure a healthy balance between online and offline time? What activities can you do that don't involve screens?

6. SCAM AWARENESS
Write down a few warning signs that might indicate a scam:

Key Takeaways

The digital world plays an important role in maintaining our connections and friendships. Social media and messaging apps allow us to keep in touch with friends, regardless of distance. However, interacting online requires extra caution and responsibility. It's vital not to share personal information publicly and to remember the same rules of friendship of trust and respect apply. Be polite, stay safe, and remember not to believe everything you see online.

FRIENDSHIPS AND CHANGES IN PUBERTY

Puberty is a significant milestone in a young girl's life, marking the transition from childhood to adulthood. It's a time of physical, emotional, and social changes, which can impact your friendships. As you navigate this new stage of your life, it's essential to understand what's happening to your body and emotions, and how these changes can affect your relationships with others.

In this chapter, we will explore the impact of puberty on friendships. You will learn how to navigate the changes and challenges that puberty may bring to your friendships. Ready? Let's get started.

Understanding Puberty

Puberty is a period of rapid growth and development, signaling the shift from childhood to young adulthood. Your body will undergo many changes, such as growing taller, starting your period, and changing shape. But puberty isn't just about physical transformation. Your emotions and feelings will also evolve during this time.

The changes you undergo during puberty can happen all at once, or slowly over time. Remember that everyone's journey through puberty is unique. You might not experience things the same way your friends do, and that's okay. These changes might make you think and feel differently about many things, and that's a normal part of growing up.

As you progress through puberty, you may notice your interests starting to change. Perhaps you used to love playing with dolls, but now you're more drawn to painting or drumming. Maybe you still enjoy music, but your taste has shifted from pop to rock. All these changes are a natural part of growing up.

CHANGING EMOTIONS

Your emotions might start changing, too. You may feel differently about relationships, goals, and even your sense of self. As you navigate these new emotions, it's essential to remember that it's okay to feel a wide range of emotions. It's part of growing up, and exploring these emotions helps shape your experiences and understanding of the world around you.

SHIFTING FRIENDSHIPS

These changes may also affect your friendships. You might find yourself drifting away from some old friends as your interests diverge or your perspectives change. That's okay. As some friendships fade, you may find new friends who share your evolving hobbies or views. In Chapter 6, we discussed how friendships can end, and that's a normal part of life. If you find yourself drifting away from some friends, remember that it's okay to let go. You can still be friendly, even if you're not as close as you once were. Managing your emotions during this time is crucial, as strong feelings can sometimes lead to disagreements.

Since puberty plays such a big role in shaping friendships, let's take a closer look at how it may impact friendships in both positive and sometimes negative ways, and what you can do to help yourself at this time.

The Impact of Puberty on Friendships

CHANGING AT DIFFERENT PACES

During puberty, your friendships will likely evolve along with the many changes you're experiencing. It's essential to remember that not everyone goes through puberty at the same pace. You and your friends may be at different stages of your puberty journeys, leading to varied interests, experiences, and emotions. It's completely natural for these differences to emerge as you grow up.

NAVIGATING CRUSHES AND FRIENDSHIPS

The hormonal changes during puberty often bring in new romantic feelings or crushes. These emotions can sometimes introduce tension, especially if two friends are attracted to the same person. In addition, dedicating more time and attention to a new crush could make your friends feel left out. While these feelings are a regular part of puberty, it's essential to balance them to maintain your existing friendships.

The Role of Self-Image in Friendships

When you enter puberty, all the physical changes you experience may make you more self-aware, or even self-conscious. This might make you sensitive to comments from your friends, or you may find that you compare yourself with your friends more often, thinking that they are prettier or smarter than you. Although it's natural to feel this way, it's crucial to remember that everyone is unique and beautiful in their own way. These feelings and insecurities can strain your relationships, so it's important to communicate with your friends and seek support if needed.

The Effects of Puberty on Friendships

Beyond the influence of self-consciousness and romantic interests, puberty can also shape your friendships in other ways. It's worth remembering that every girl's journey through puberty is different. As a result, the effects of puberty on your friendships will be unique to your situation. These changes can strengthen or weaken your friendships.

Some Friendships Will Grow Stronger

Shared experiences during puberty, such as navigating the same challenges and emotions, can bring you closer together with some friends. These mutual experiences form a solid foundation, often making your friendships even stronger than before.

Some Friendships Will Fade

On the other hand, puberty may also lead to some friendships fading away. If you find that you and a friend don't share the same interests anymore, or if you argue a lot, it might be time to reevaluate the friendship. It's essential to recognize that some friendships might not survive the changes experienced during puberty, and that's okay.

New Friendships Will Bloom

As your interests and views change during puberty, you'll probably meet new people who share these interests and ideas. This is a great chance to make new friends. Many of these new friends will help shape who you become as a teenager and young adult, and some of them might even be your friends for the rest of your life.

Managing Changes in Friendships During Puberty

Puberty can bring about changes in your friendships. You might not always see these changes as they happen, but one day, you may realize that a friendship has changed, for better or worse. It's important to remember that your friends are also experiencing puberty and will be dealing with their own emotions and feelings during this time.

Even though everyone's experience of puberty is unique, we all go through it, and many of the changes and feelings are common. Keeping this in mind can help you relate better to your friends as you all navigate the challenges of puberty. Here are four strategies to help you manage changes in your friendships during puberty:

1. Open Communication

Talk openly with your friends about your feelings and thoughts. It can be hard to share your emotions, but it's key to building trust and understanding in your friendships. By opening up, you make it easier for your friends to share their feelings with you, too. Remember, they may be experiencing similar emotions and will appreciate having someone to talk to.

2. Understanding

Try to be more understanding when your friends' behavior, interests, or opinions change. They're going through puberty, too, and may have mood swings, lowered self-esteem, or conflicting emotions that affect their actions. Keep in mind that you may also have times when you struggle with similar feelings. Being understanding and giving each other the space to grow is vital for maintaining healthy friendships during puberty.

3. Patience

Being patient with your friends is crucial, especially when you have differing opinions. It's natural to feel confused or uncertain during puberty, as the physical and emotional changes can be overwhelming. You may also become more sensitive to criticism. Being patient makes it easier for your friends to feel understood and supported. In return, they'll likely extend the same patience to you.

4. Empathy

Empathy is the ability to understand and share someone else's feelings, even if they're not your own. Show empathy When your friends feel emotional, confused, or frustrated. While you may not share their feelings, you can understand what it's like to experience strong emotions for no apparent reason. Demonstrating empathy helps your friends feel supported and valued, even if your interests change or your friendship wanes.

Understanding how puberty affects friendships is essential for navigating this period of change. The following case study and questions will help you see the impact of puberty on friendships in real life. You can also complete the activity, where you'll write about your thoughts and emotions to process and embrace the changes you're experiencing during puberty. Best of luck!

Kayla and Madison

Kayla and Madison have been best friends since kindergarten. They've always been close, sharing everything from secrets to favorite games. But when they started middle school, things began to change. Madison started growing taller, getting pimples, and even needing a bra. On the other hand, Kayla didn't notice any big changes in her body.

Madison's other friends, who were also going through these changes, started forming their own group. They often talked about their new experiences, making Kayla feel left out and a little lost. She wasn't part of these new conversations and felt like she didn't belong anymore.

The distance between Kayla and Madison kept growing, and both of them felt sad about it. Finally, Kayla decided to talk to Madison about feeling left out.

During their chat, Madison reassured Kayla that their friendship meant the world to her, and it didn't matter who was taller or had more pimples. They promised to support each other through all the weird and wonderful changes that come with growing up.

Answer the following questions about Kayla and Madison's friendship.

1. How did Kayla and Madison handle the changes in their friendship when they started going through puberty at different times?

   _____

   _____

   _____

2. Why is it important to be understanding when your friends go through changes, even if you're not experiencing them yet?

   _____

   _____

   _____

3. What are some ways you can show support for a friend who feels left out because they're experiencing puberty at a different pace?

   _____

   _____

   _____

Activity: Journaling About Changes

As we have already explored, puberty is a time of changes, and sometimes it can feel overwhelming, especially with everything that's going on. Keeping a journal where you can write about your feelings can be a helpful way to express these emotions and make sense of them.

You don't always have to share your thoughts and feelings with others if you're not ready, or if you'd rather keep them private. Writing them down can give you the chance to explore your emotions without having to share them, and that's perfectly okay. In fact, it can help you process and better understand what you're going through, giving you a mature perspective on your feelings and experiences.

Writing might not be everyone's preferred way to process things, but it's definitely worth giving it a try. Journaling can give you a sense of control and a space to reflect on your thoughts and feelings. What will your journal entry be today?

Here are some simple prompts to help you get started:

1. Changes I've noticed in my interests lately...

2. How my friendships have evolved during puberty...

3. Emotions that were strong for me today...

4. My thoughts on the physical changes I'm going through...

5. Goals I want to set for myself...

6. Challenges I faced today and how I felt about them...

7. The best moment of my day was...

8. Three things I'm thankful for today...

9. What I hope for in the coming weeks...

DAILY JOURNAL

Date:

M T W T F S S

Key Takeaways

Puberty has a big impact on your friendships. Sometimes, the changes you go through during puberty, both physical and emotional, can either strengthen your friendships or cause them to fade away. As your interests change, you might also find yourself making new friends who share your new interests. Remember, everyone's experience of puberty is unique. By showing empathy, understanding, communicating openly, and being patient with your friends, you'll be able to support and care for them as they navigate their own puberty journeys.

FOSTERING KINDNESS AND RESPECT IN FRIENDSHIPS

Kindness and respect are essential for healthy relationships, whether with family, friends, or romantic partners.

In this chapter, we'll explore how to cultivate these qualities in your friendships. We'll define kindness and respect, explain their importance in lasting friendships, and offer practical tips on how to practice them.

We'll also take a closer look at a real-life example of a friendship where kindness and respect are front and center. This case study will help you understand how these qualities play out in day-to-day life and make friendships stronger.

Understanding Kindness and Respect

Kindness involves showing genuine care and helping others, regardless of their background or what they can offer in return. In friendships, kindness means being there for your friends, celebrating their achievements, and listening with empathy. Treating friends as equals who are deserving of love and respect is key.

Respect is about valuing others for who they are, even if you don't always agree with their opinions or values. Respecting friends means honoring their feelings and choices, creating a trust-based foundation in your friendship. This trust helps you handle disagreements constructively.

Being kind and respectful contributes to strong friendships and sets the standard for how you want to be treated. "Treat others as you want to be treated" remains a timeless guideline. Kindness and respect also benefit society, fostering community, understanding, and acceptance.

The Importance of Kindness and Respect in Friendships

As you go through puberty, face peer pressure, and experience shifts in interests, it's crucial to treat your friends with kindness and respect.

Let's explore why these qualities are essential in teenage friendships and beyond.

- **Resolving Conflict**: In your teenage years, conflicts can arise more often due to the pressure to fit in and the formation of strong opinions. Treating your friends with kindness and respect makes you more likely to approach disagreements with empathy, valuing friendship over minor disputes.

- **Improving Communication**: Respect involves listening, while kindness requires speaking with patience. Practicing these qualities in your friendships creates a comfortable environment for open conversations, fostering trust and facilitating honest communication.

- **Strengthening Bonds**: Kindness and respect create a trusting atmosphere where your friends feel comfortable sharing their lives with you. When you show respect and kindness, your friends are more likely to confide in you and seek your support in difficult times, which deepens your friendship.

The Importance of Mutual Respect

Nurturing strong friendships requires mutual kindness and respect. Showing your friends respect and kindness is crucial, but you deserve the same in return.

Mutual respect means valuing each other's thoughts and feelings, even when you disagree. Differences can introduce new perspectives and enrich a friendship, provided both friends treat each other's opinions with respect and understanding. By fostering mutual respect and kindness, you create a safe space for open sharing and deeper connections.

Promoting Kindness and Respect

Being kind and respectful to your friends sounds pretty straightforward, but it can sometimes be challenging to know exactly how to put it into action. Here are four ways you can show kindness and respect in your friendships.

1. Expressing Gratitude

Show your friends that you value and appreciate them by expressing gratitude. Say thank you for their support, be there for them when they need a helping hand, and treat them in a way that reflects your appreciation for their friendship.

2. Offering Help

Being there for your friends when they need help, no matter how small the task, is a clear sign of kindness. If your friend is moving to a new place, offer to help pack their belongings or transport boxes. Being supportive and caring during their times of need strengthens your friendship and showcases your genuine concern.

3. Open Communication

Open and honest communication is vital in any friendship. Whether you're giving a compliment or addressing an issue, clear communication promotes mutual respect, kindness, and trust. Just as your friends should feel comfortable discussing things with you, you should also feel comfortable addressing your concerns. Friendship doesn't mean you'll always agree, but you should be able to communicate your disagreements with respect and care.

4. Respecting Personal Boundaries

Recognizing and respecting your friends' boundaries is key to showing kindness and respect. If your friend has asked for space or expressed discomfort with a particular topic, honor their wishes without pressuring them. Similarly, a respectful friend will respect your boundaries without pressuring you to do something you're uncomfortable with.

When you understand and practice mutual respect and kindness, you can apply these principles in real-life situations. Below, you'll find a case study about two individuals who treated each other with kindness and respect. You will also find a kindness and respect challenge that you and your friends can participate in to further cultivate these essential qualities in your relationships.

Case Study:

Lily and Sam

Lily and Sam were childhood friends who lived in the same neighborhood. They played together every day and shared everything. However, as they entered high school, they started to drift apart due to their different interests and groups of friends.

During this time, Sam's parents divorced, and she struggled to cope with the changes in her life. She felt lonely and isolated. Lily noticed the change and decided to reach out.

Lily made a point of sitting with Sam at lunch, listening to her concerns, and offering support. She also invited her to join her group of friends. Her friends welcomed Sam with open arms.

Sam appreciated Lily's gesture and started to feel less alone. Over time, their friendship was rekindled, and Sam learned the importance of being there for someone when they needed it the most. As they moved through high school, they remained close friends, always valuing their shared history and the kindness they had shown to each other.

Answer the following questions about Lily *and Sam's friendship.*

1. **How did Lily demonstrate kindness and respect towards Sam?**

   _____

   _____

2. **Why was Lily's support so crucial for Sam during her parents' divorce?**

   _____

   _____

   _____

3. **How did Lily's actions impact their friendship and Sam's well-being?**

   _____

   _____

4. **In what ways can you show kindness and respect to friends who may be going through a tough time, even if you've drifted apart?**

   _____

   _____

   _____

Activity: Kindness and Respect Challenge

This activity aims to help you improve your friendships by intentionally practicing kindness and showing respect towards your friends. You might be surprised by the positive impact it can have!

DECIDE ON A TIME FRAME
Choose a specific period for your challenge, such as two weeks or a month. The grid provided has space for 14 days, but you can adjust it according to your chosen time frame.

PERFORM ACTS OF KINDNESS
Each day, carry out at least one act of kindness towards a friend. It could be something small, like helping them with a task or offering a compliment, or something bigger, like supporting them through a challenging time.

DISPLAY RESPECT
In addition to your act of kindness, make a conscious effort to display respect in your interactions with friends each day. This could include listening actively, acknowledging their feelings, or respecting their boundaries.

RECORD YOUR ACTIONS
Use the grid template provided to track your acts of kindness and displays of respect. In the "Act of Kindness" and "Display of Respect" columns, jot down your specific actions for each day.

REFLECT ON YOUR EXPERIENCES
In the "Observations and Notes" column, write down any notable experiences, reactions from your friends, or personal reflections related to your actions. Consider how these actions may have influenced your friendships.

EVALUATE YOUR CHALLENGE
At the end of your chosen time frame, review your grid and reflect on the overall impact of your actions on your friendships and your personal growth. Did you notice any positive changes in your relationships? What did you learn about the importance of kindness and respect?

Remember, this challenge is an opportunity for self-reflection and growth in your friendships. Be genuine in your actions and enjoy positively impacting your relationships through kindness and respect.

 Key Takeaways

Kindness and respect are essential ingredients in any successful friendship. These qualities not only help resolve conflicts and improve communication, but also strengthen the bond between friends. You can cultivate kindness and respect in your friendships by expressing thanks to your friends, helping them, and openly communicating with them. Choosing kindness and respect can transform your relationships and create the foundations of fulfilling, lifelong friendships.

Challenge Log

Act of kindness	Display of respect	Observations & Notes

DAY 1

DAY 2

DAY 3

DAY 4

DAY 5

DAY 6

DAY 7

CONCLUSION

Congratulations on finishing this book! You've embarked on a fantastic journey into the world of friendships, and now you're armed with all the knowledge you need to be the best friend you can be. Real friendships are built on respect, trust, empathy, and kindness. Each chapter has given you the tools to navigate friendships in your teenage years and beyond, whether they're in person or online.

You now know how to approach new people, manage different personalities within your group of friends, and overcome challenges like jealousy and peer pressure. You've even learned how to cope with the loss of a friend and how to handle the changes that come with growing up.

This is just the beginning! Your challenge now is to put all this knowledge into action in your own life. As you do, you'll become a better friend, attract better friends, and keep the good friends you already have. So go out there, embrace the lessons you've learned, and build those strong, positive, happy friendships.

You've got this!

BEMBERTON
BOOKS

THANKS
FOR READING MY
BOOK!

I appreciate you picking this guide to help your tween girl understand and navigate the exciting yet sometimes puzzling journey of puberty.

I would be so grateful if you could take a moment to leave an honest review or a star rating on Amazon.
(A star rating is just a couple of clicks away.)

By leaving a review, you'll help other parents discover this valuable resource for their own children. Thank you!

To leave a review & help spread the word

SCAN
HERE

A Tween Girl's Guide
to
Puberty
The Complete Body and Mind
Handbook for Young Girls

If you enjoyed this book, I think you'll love the first book in the series: "**A Tween Girl's Guide to Puberty.**"

Filled with practical tips, relatable examples, and simple illustrations, this guide empowers young girls with the knowledge they need to confidently embrace and savor their unique journeys.

REFERENCES

10. Cherry, K. (2023, March 11). *The Big Five Personality Traits*. Verywell Mind. https://www.verywellmind.com/the-big-five-personality-dimensions-2795422

11. Degges-White, S. (2017, November 1). *Confronting Conflict With Friends*. Psychology Today. https://www.psychologytoday.com/za/blog/lifetime-connections/201711/confronting-conflict-friends

12. Dowshen, S. (2015). *Everything You Wanted to Know About Puberty (for Teens)*. Kidshealth.org. https://kidshealth.org/en/teens/puberty.html

13. *Dr. Seuss Quotes About Being Different*. (n.d.). A-Z Quotes. Retrieved June 30, 2023, from https://www.azquotes.com/author/13348-Dr_Seuss/tag/being-different

14. *Healthy Relationships in Adolescence*. (2022). Office of Population Affairs. https://opa.hhs.gov/adolescent-health/healthy-relationships-adolescence

15. *How to be respectful and respected*. (n.d.). Kids Helpline. https://kidshelpline.com.au/teens/issues/all-about-respect

16. Miguel, M. (2018, May 7). *Define Friend: A Good Understanding of the Friend Definition.* Betterhelp. https://www.betterhelp.com/advice/friendship/define-friend-a-good-understanding-of-the-friend-definition/

17. Nurick, Jennifer. (2021, November 8). *Healthy vs. Unhealthy Friendships.* https://jennynurick.com/healthy-vs-unhealthy-friendships/

18. *Our Definition of Bullying.* (n.d.). Anti-Bullying Alliance. https://anti-bullyingalliance.org.uk/tools-information/all-about-bullying/understanding-bullying/definition

19. *Personality Test.* (n.d.). Attitude. https://www.attitude.org.nz/personality-test

20. *7 Body-Language Hacks to Try When Meeting New People.* (2017, August 7). Entrepreneur. https://www.entrepreneur.com/leadership/7-body-language-hacks-to-try-when-meeting-new-people

21. *What Is Kindness?* (n.d.). Kindness Is Everything. https://www.kindnessiseverything.com/faqs/what-is-kindness/

Made in the USA
Middletown, DE
02 May 2024

53761154R00095